LEADERSHIP
IN
100 QUOTES

METRO BOOKS
New York

An Imprint of Sterling Publishing Co., Inc.
1166 Avenue of the Americas
New York, NY 10036

METRO BOOKS and the distinctive Metro Books logo are
registered trademarks of Sterling Publishing Co., Inc.

© 2018 Quarto Publishing plc

All rights reserved. No part of this publication may be reproduced, stored in a
retrieval system, or transmitted in any form or by any means (including electronic,
mechanical, photocopying, recording, or otherwise) without prior written
permission from the publisher.

ISBN 978-1-4351-6780-3

For information about custom editions, special sales, and premium
and corporate purchases, please contact Sterling Special Sales
at 800-805-5489 or specialsales@sterlingpublishing.com

Manufactured in China

2 4 6 8 10 9 7 5 3 1

sterlingpublishing.com

Design by Tony Seddon

LEADERSHIP
IN
100 QUOTES

CHARLES PHILLIPS

METRO BOOKS
New York

INTRODUCTION

Are leaders born, or made? Can you teach yourself to be a good leader? I firmly believe that women and men make themselves into good leaders through a combination of learning, self-discipline, and hard work. Learning in this context involves listening to others and modeling your behavior on their example. We have all likely encountered one or two excellent leaders in the course of our education and working lives and have been given the opportunity to undertake some free leadership training. Think back or consider current colleagues who impress you. What works for them? How do they build and maintain loyalty? What do they avoid in their dealings with staff? Then look at yourself. How are you like the best leaders? How could you change to model your behavior more closely on the way they work and manage teams?

You have in your hands an essential complement to this process—a leadership skills handbook. Listen to some of the greatest leaders in history and of the present day. From Homer in the 8th century BCE through to TED talks and start-up leaders in the 21st century, we dip into almost 3,000 years of leadership expertise.

On the way we take in the very best. You will find advice from the most powerful generals, including Alexander the Great, Napoleon, and Norman Schwarzkopf, as well as penetrating insights into how to conduct ourselves from literary greats including Shakespeare, Hemingway, and Alice Walker. Guidance from political leaders like John F. Kennedy, Indira Gandhi, and Barack Obama is complemented by profound statements from philosophers and religious thinkers such as Socrates, Martin Luther King, Jr., and Pope Francis. There's still room for leadership gurus like John C. Maxwell, peerless sporting managers like John McGraw, campaigners such as Emmeline Pankhurst and Rosa Parks, and brilliant lights of the entertainment firmament like Oprah. Others featured in this book are controversial figures with disputed legacies, although the dubiousness of the cause does not negate the quality of their leadership.

In almost every example, the leadership greats quoted in this book support the argument that leadership can be—and needs to be—learned. Some voices, like that of the ancient Greek statesman Pericles, do make us consider whether leadership qualities might be inherent. Pericles' insight (see page 15) homes in on the importance of being a gifted speaker—the man renowned as one of history's greatest orators focused on the necessity of being able to convince others. Yet the great majority of others stress above all the importance of self-inquiry and hard work in making yourself a leader. As leaders go, there are not many better than Vince Lombardi (see page 121), celebrated as the greatest ever American football coach. His view? "Leaders are not born, they are made."

So how do we make ourselves into great leaders? By being brave, solving problems, holding to our vision, and being innovative. By having self-belief, setting aside doubts and getting to it. We should ensure we have good advisors and listen to them. We should pick our battles, not trying to win every single struggle, but only the most important ones. We should give others hope. Several voices in the pages that follow encourage us to be outwardly focused, to think of others, even while we are being leaders. From Laozi to Bill Gates and Sheryl Sandberg, they stress that the best leaders aim to focus on drawing out the qualities of the people they lead. Perhaps the last word should go to one of the towering leaders of the 20th century, Nelson Mandela, and his seemingly counterintuitive advice that we should "lead from behind and put others in front."

Be both a speaker of words and a doer of deeds.

HOMER
8th century BCE

SOURCE: The *Iliad*
DATE: ca. 750 BCE
FIELD: Epic poetry

This advice is given in Homer's epic poem the *Iliad* to Achilles, the greatest warrior in the Mycenaean Greek army that besieged the city of Troy for ten years in ca. 1250 BCE. The speaker, Phoenix son of Amyntor, is a much older follower of Achilles, who had helped raise the young hero.

We know very little for sure about Homer, save that the ancient Greeks identified him as the author of two great poems—the *Iliad*, about the legendary Trojan War, and the *Odyssey*, about the long journey home of Greek hero Odysseus. Both were probably composed in the 8th century BCE. Tradition has it that Homer was blind and lived on the Greek island of Chios. He probably did not write down his great works but performed them—the word he uses for poet means "singer." The poems are founding works of literature in the Western world, and from the ancient Greeks on, people have seen them as a great source of inspiration and moral guidance. Alexander the Great supposedly slept with a copy of the *Iliad* under his pillow every night.

Phoenix's advice to Achilles emphasizes the importance of words, and the power of language to convince and inspire followers. Yet he also encourages those in charge of groups to lead by example—to show and do, as well as tell. Achilles goes on to prove the worth of deeds by winning a famous victory in single combat over Trojan warrior Hector. Leaders who are doers inspire achievement in others.

A leader is best when people barely know he exists. When his work is done, his aim fulfilled, they will say: "We did it ourselves."

LAOZI
6th century BCE

SOURCE: *Daodejing*
DATE: ca. 550 BCE
FIELD: Civil service

Ancient Chinese philosopher Laozi delivered this insight on leadership in his venerated work the *Daodejing* (*Classic of the Way of Virtue*). According to tradition, Laozi was a diviner and keeper of records at the royal court of the Zhou kings, probably in the 6th century BCE, and in the *Daodejing* proposed a way of living designed to bring peace and harmony to a land troubled by conflict. Although most modern scholars doubt that the *Daodejing* was written by a single author and many consider Laozi an apocryphal figure, the work he reputedly wrote is the founding document of the Chinese religious-philosophical movement of Daoism. Its adherents seek to follow the *Dao* ("Way") and aim for *wu wei* ("not acting"), meaning not that they do nothing, but that they allow events to take their natural course.

This understanding casts an unusual but valuable light on leadership. Sometimes it is useful to do less. Take a step back and allow events to develop; a lighter touch can mean that conflicts and quarrels dissipate. A leader can keep her hand on the tiller while apparently handing over control to subordinates, and this kind of leadership develops independence and self-confidence in workers, students, or other followers. Here the leader is not seeking praise or glory, but the realization of her goals. As the quote suggests, this form of leadership has two targets: first, to achieve the set goals; and second, to empower the followers. The leader's "work is done, his aim fulfilled," but the followers congratulate one another—"We did it ourselves."

In **ANGER** we should refrain both from *speech* and *action.*

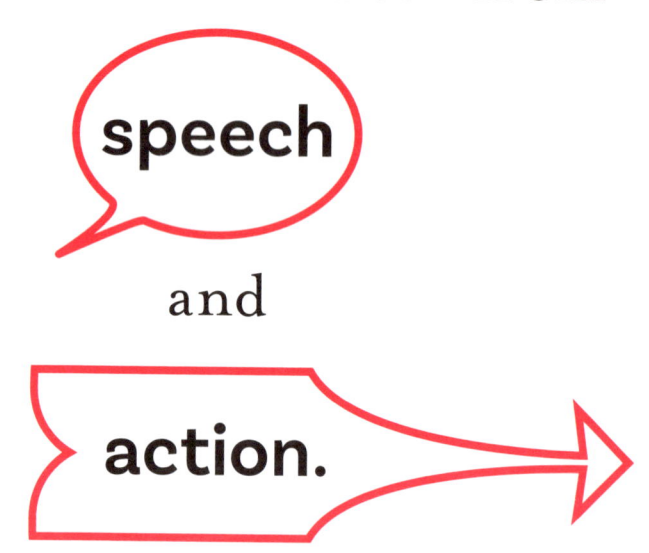

PYTHAGORAS
ca. 570–ca. 490 BCE

SOURCE: Reported saying
DATE: ca. 525 BCE
FIELD: Mathematics

Pythagoras was a groundbreaking mathematician and natural scientist, and reputedly the first man to declare himself a philosopher, or "lover of wisdom." He left his native Samos, a Greek island in the eastern Aegean Sea, to establish a teaching academy at Crotone in southern Italy. His name is associated above all with the Pythagorean theorem in geometry, a rule concerning the right-angled or 90-degree triangle—according to tradition, he and his followers, the Pythagoreans, discovered this, although modern scholars have proven that it was already known hundreds of years earlier in Babylonia and India. Pythagoras' ideas influenced the great ancient Greek philosophers Plato and Aristotle, and the entire history of mathematics and Western thought.

Here this great teacher advises us as leaders to hold off acting and speaking when we are angry. Anger can short-circuit our rational mind, so that we say things to the wrong people, or in the wrong tone, or at the wrong time, or simply say something we do not mean. As well, anger can push us to lash out physically, make a rash business judgment, or fire someone we value. Of course, anger can be a force for good. It can be the energy that drives us to effect change. However, to have a good effect it must be under our control, and that means we have followed Pythagoras' advice; we have not acted in the heat of the moment and are using a sense of indignation in a controlled manner.

When it is obvious that
the goals cannot be reached,
don't adjust the goals,
adjust the action steps.

CONFUCIUS
551–479 BCE

SOURCE: Reported saying
DATE: ca. 500 BCE
FIELD: Civil service

Chinese political theorist and philosopher Confucius argued for respect, obedience, and order, and his teachings have had a profound influence on the Chinese way of life for more than 2,500 years. Born in a relatively modest social position in 551 BCE, he worked in government jobs, including as the manager of stables and a granary, but dedicated himself to learning. He mastered Chinese traditions in history and the arts, especially poetry, before becoming a teacher in his 30s. He stressed the importance of personal development though education and public service, and he later worked as a magistrate and minister of justice.

Confucius argued that education should be available to all and that everyone can develop their skills and capacity for excellence, and he taught leadership, developing an educational course in the humanities for people set to become leaders. The words in his quote encourage leaders to be persistent in seeking to attain their goals. The path to success is not always straightforward or easy, to put it mildly; but that certainly does not mean leaders should give up. Keep your eyes on the prize, as they say, but adjust your thinking on how to get there. Leaders can play a crucial role here in managing disappointment at setbacks and overseeing a calm but productive reappraisal of what Confucius calls "the action steps." A key leadership element is developing judgment and insight to determine when is the right time to lay one approach aside and develop another.

A man who has knowledge but lacks power to express it clearly is no better off than if he never had any ideas at all.

PERICLES
ca. 495–429 BCE

SOURCE: Pericles' oration, reported by Thucydides
DATE: 431 BCE
FIELDS: Statecraft/the military

Ancient Greek statesman and general Pericles delivered these words in a stirring speech he made to commemorate Athenians who had been killed in the first year of the Peloponnesian War (431–404 BCE) between Athens and the rival Greek city-state of Sparta. The speech was described by Thucydides, who wrote an eight-volume history of the Peloponnesian war that is praised as the first work of "modern history"—an account that analyzes causes and effects and sets out to be impartial in its analysis. Pericles was at the end of a great career (he died two years later, in 429 BCE) and in this funeral oration of 431 BCE spoke with the authority of experience and of a man responsible for building the Parthenon temple and fostering democracy in Athens.

Pericles was famous for his skill as an orator. As he says here, leaders need to be communicators. There is no point having great ideas if you are unable to express them and convince others—you might just as well not bother developing the ideas at all. For some people, communication comes naturally and easily. For others, it is more of a challenge, yet training is available. You can learn how to speak well in public, how to write effectively, and how to develop your skills in using social media and the latest interactive means of communication. The ability to communicate is a preeminent leadership skill, for to lead you need to be able not only to make decisions decisively but also to convince others you have called it right.

Let him who would move the world first move himself.

06

SOCRATES
ca. 470–399 BCE

SOURCE: Socrates' teaching, reported by Plato
DATE: ca. 410 BCE
FIELD: Philosophy

Ancient Greek philosopher Socrates, active in Athens in the 5th century BCE, was famous for his statement, "The unexamined life is not worth living" and for the so-called "Socratic method" of debate, whereby two people talking to one another use a series of questions to draw out assumptions and establish definitions. He used this to investigate the morality and ethics of his contemporaries in Athens. Most of what we know about him comes through the writing of his pupils and disciples, Plato and Xenophon. Plato says Socrates believed that no one desires to do wrong and that when they go astray it is through ignorance.

His advice here seems to mean: Lead by example. He suggests that you have to bring about in yourself the change you want to see in other people; as a leader, you have to model the behavior you think is needed. If you want your team to improve its timekeeping, then you need to be punctual yourself; if you want to see streamlined procedures and decision-making, then you need to hone your own way of working. We all know from experience that it is generally easier to change by emulating behavior than by consciously following instructions. You might interpret Socrates' "move" to mean "motivate," in which case his insight is just as powerful: To motivate your team, you need first to motivate yourself. You need to embody enthusiasm and drive, and you will become a focus for team members' energy. You carry followers along with you, rather than needing to direct and manage their behavior.

He who has never learned to **obey** cannot be a good commander.

ARISTOTLE
384–322 BCE

SOURCE: *Politics*
DATE: ca. 350 BCE
FIELD: Philosophy

One of the key figures in the history of Western philosophy, Aristotle laid the foundations for generations of later thinkers. He was born in Macedonia in 384 BCE, studied under fellow-philosopher Plato at his Academy in Athens for two decades, then tutored the future Alexander the Great for three years, before returning to Athens to open his own school in the Lyceum, a temple to the god Apollo in Athens. Aristotle was a pioneer in logic and zoology, and taught also botany, biology, chemistry, psychology, ethics, and metaphysics.

His advice on leadership makes sense first and foremost in a military context, where discipline and effectiveness depend on orders being obeyed without dispute. To deploy his authority to best effect, a military commander needs experience of having received and followed orders—he needs to have learned to obey. Because he has received orders in the past, he will know the best way to frame and deliver orders now. In business and other fields, discipline is also key. Team members and followers will watch to see whether their leader's behavior is in line with the business' identity. Leaders who lack discipline, who are not obedient to the culture of the workplace, may struggle. Self-discipline, a key leadership attribute, can also be seen as an aspect of obedience—if a leader wants to establish rules for her team, she needs to follow them herself as much as possible. Followers who see a leader commit to a goal, and put personal benefits aside, will be willing to do the same, to work for the common good.

I do not steal victory.

ALEXANDER THE GREAT
356–323 BCE

SOURCE: Plutarch's *Life of Alexander*
DATE: September 30, 331 BCE
FIELD: Generalship

The most famous general of the ancient world, Macedonian prince Alexander the Great conquered an empire of more than 2 million square miles (5 million sq km) before his death in Babylon at the age of just 32. He was an immensely talented commander who led his troops by example, and also a thoughtful, well-educated man who had been tutored at the Macedonian royal court by the philosopher Aristotle. In the course of his conquests, he defeated the mighty Persian Empire of the Achaemenid monarchs and, according to the ancient Greek historian Plutarch, he said the words quoted opposite when his leading general Parmenio suggested they attack the army of the Persian ruler Darius by night. Alexander instead waited, and the following day he won a decisive victory in the Battle of Gaugamela on October 1, 331 BCE, driving Darius to flight and the Persian army to panic.

For us as leaders the lesson of these words is: Be seen to compete fairly and honorably. A victory won by underhand means may bring short-term and personal benefits but undermines your status as a leader, because cutting corners and cheating suggests you lack confidence to win fair and square. Parmenio made the suggestion because he saw the Macedonian army was greatly outnumbered; Alexander ruled that he and his troops get rest ahead of a battle the next day. By contrast, it is reported, Darius suspected a night attack and kept his troops in a state of readiness all night. Alexander's confidence paid off and the well-rested Macedonian army roared to victory.

Wise leaders generally have wise counselors, because it takes a wise person themselves to distinguish them.

DIOGENES OF SINOPE
Died ca. 320 BCE

SOURCE: Diogenes' teaching
DATE: ca. 320 BCE
FIELDS: Education/philosophy

In the 4th century BCE the thinker and teacher Diogenes, born in Sinope in what is now northern Turkey, lived according to the Cynic school of philosophy. He was outspoken and shameless in rejecting convention and seeking a simple, "natural" way of life. Driven into exile, he settled in Athens, where he was known by Aristotle. He argued that people could train themselves to be independent and happy through asceticism, a life rejecting luxury and normal customs—the word "asceticism" derives from the Greek *askesis* ("training").

His comment here suggests you can tell how good a leader is by judging the quality of her assistants. A leader needs to be wise to choose her immediate helpers and subordinates well, he says; so if you encounter impressive support staff around a leader, you can be confident the leader will be accomplished. Equally, a person setting out as a leader should devote time and care to choosing her team. What are "wise counselors"? They are not "yes-men." They will tell you you are wrong or urge you to delay a course of action if necessary, and they will expect you to listen. Of course, you may decide to reject their input, and leadership often involves difficult feedback or making lonely decisions; as former British prime minister Tony Blair says (see page 145), "The art of leadership is saying no, not saying yes." Yet a good leader is careful of her team and knows she can rely on them. Great leaders have great teams around them.

A good general not only sees the way to victory; he also knows when victory is impossible.

POLYBIUS
ca. 200–118 BCE

SOURCE: *The Histories*
DATE: ca. 146 BCE
FIELD: History

Ancient Greek historian and statesman Polybius wrote a 40-book history covering the rise of Rome to the status of a world power in the years 264–146 BCE. Only five books of this massive work survive, but they give a vivid account of Rome's long war against the North African power of Carthage. Polybius knew Rome from the inside, having been taken hostage following Rome's defeat of Perseus of Macedonia in 168 BCE and held for 18 years, and he was also an eyewitness to the Sack of Carthage in 146 BCE.

Polybius' statement focuses on the value of strategic judgment. The best leaders know that some battles cannot be won: A general may see that attacking an enemy in a particular position will lead to defeat, so will move his troops to approach differently. A business leader may see that going head to head with a rival for a particular contract is likely to fail, so will wait or back up and try a different approach. Your authority suffers if you do not show good judgment in terms of what is achievable. People will not follow a leader blindly into a doomed enterprise. Sometimes you accept a smaller setback on the way to a larger victory; good leaders keep the overall goal in mind. A very important part of leadership is the ability to maintain morale when things may seem to be going wrong and to keep followers focused on the long-term results. In interviews, great leaders often describe how they recovered from setbacks.

Anyone can hold the helm when the sea is calm.

PUBLILIUS SYRUS
1st century BCE

SOURCE: *Sententiae*
DATE: ca. 50 BCE
FIELD: Entertainment

Brought to Italy as a slave from his native Syria, Publilius Syrus made his name as a deviser of mimed entertainments and is known most of all for his *sententiae*, or moral maxims. These were taken from his mime shows and gathered in a collection that was prized by later writers. Another of the sententiae is the well-known proverb, "A rolling stone gathers no moss."

The maxim opposite, number 385 of the 700-strong collection, implies that good leaders really prove their worth when challenges arise. When the sea is calm, then it is hardly challenging to be at the helm, but when it is rough, it is a struggle for the captain to keep the vessel on course. If team members fall out over strategy, work practices, or personal matters, then it is your task as leader to act swiftly and be even-handed in restoring calm. If you and your team suffer a setback, then it is up to you to maintain morale and model a positive outlook. Cooperation of team members will be needed when times are tough—imagine the captain calling on the crew to help in the teeth of the storm, and afterward, when the ship makes it through, everyone feels great and their confidence receives a boost. Such trying circumstances can boost team morale and the standing of the leader. Perhaps it is worth also noting that calm seas can conceal corals or sandbanks and that, for all Publilius says, you must remain alert when things seem to be going well.

THEY CAN BECAUSE THEY *THINK* THEY CAN.

VIRGIL
70–19 BCE

SOURCE: The *Aeneid*
DATE: 29–19 BCE
FIELD: Epic poetry

Roman poet Virgil's 12-book epic poem the *Aeneid*, begun in ca. 30 BCE, tells the story of Aeneas, hero of the Trojan War and forefather of the Roman race. He is considered an ancestor of Romulus and Remus, the legendary founders of Rome. Virgil, generally seen as the greatest of all Roman poets, aims in his poem to justify and celebrate the glorious destiny of Rome to rule the known world.

The line opposite comes from Book V of the poem and refers to the crew of a ship as they pursue another ahead of them in a contest of strength and athleticism. They are gaining and their success fuels their belief that they can overtake the other vessel. It is a powerful insight for leaders into the strength of self-belief, not only a leader's belief in herself, but also the self-belief she can foster in members of the team working for her. People achieve more if they feel confident—look at how sports teams go on winning runs; the fact that they have been winning helps them win again. This phrase was the motto of 19 Squadron of the British Royal Air Force, which performed airborne heroics to intercept and turn back the invading bombers of the German Luftwaffe during the Battle of Britain in 1940—a convincing demonstration of the power of self-belief to drive people right up to and even potentially beyond the limits of their ability. As a leader, be sure to develop your team's confidence and drive through praise and by modeling self-discipline and confidence.

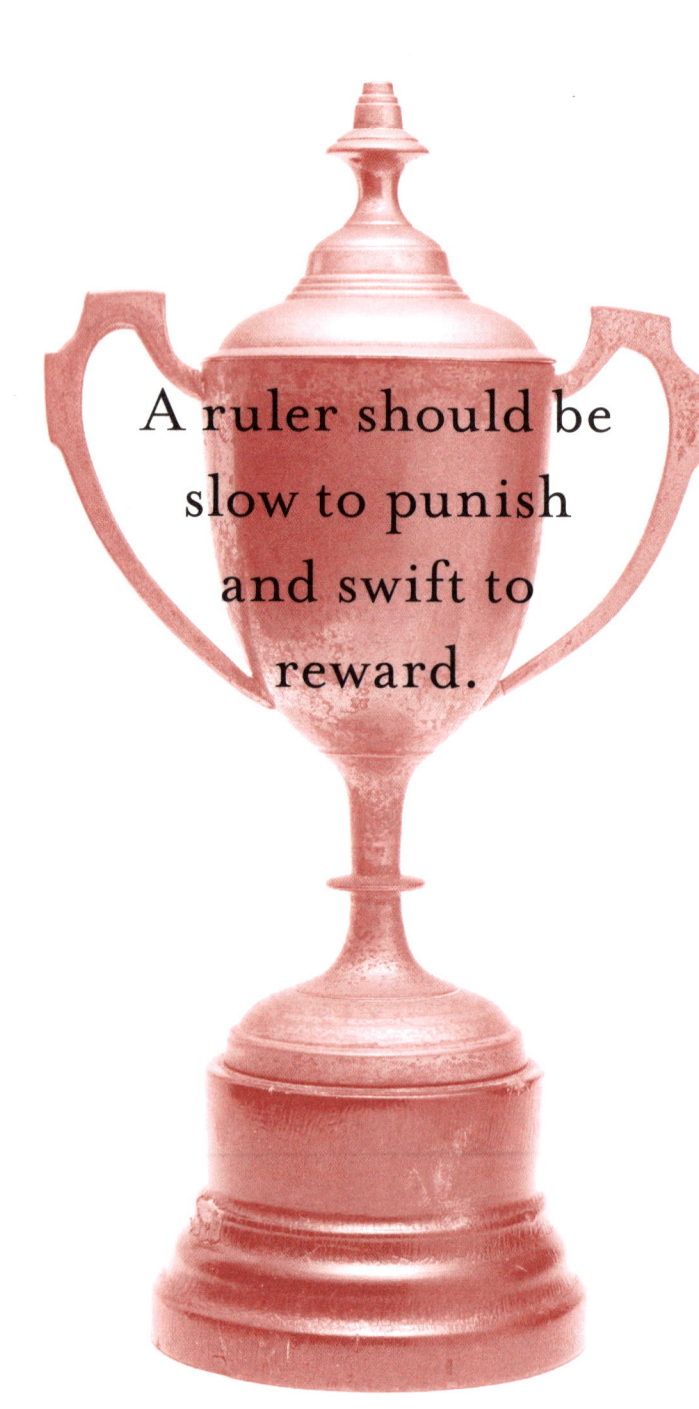

A ruler should be slow to punish and swift to reward.

OVID
43 BCE–17 CE

SOURCE: Reported saying
DATE: ca. 1 CE
FIELD: Poetry

The works of Roman poet Ovid, which include *Art of Love* and *Metamorphoses*, were a major influence on Geoffrey Chaucer, William Shakespeare, and other important authors. He was born in rural Italy and studied and settled in Rome, where he was successful as a poet, but he ended his life in exile in Tomis on the Black Sea (modern Constanta in Romania) after being banished for unknown reasons by Emperor Augustus. Modern scholars think he probably offended Augustus by becoming embroiled somehow in a scandal surrounding the emperor's granddaughter Julia, who had an affair with Roman senator Decimus Junius Silanus.

The ruler who banished Ovid—the first Roman emperor, Augustus—was an autocrat who ruled with absolute authority and was severe in his judgments. He also banished his granddaughter Julia and her mother, his own daughter. The poet's advice in the quote opposite, however, urges a different style of leadership, one that is gentle in reprimanding shortfalls and looks to support the good points in your team members' performance. It is necessary to tread the fine line between being lenient with a follower's shortfalls in a way that builds morale, and being too soft. No one would encourage a leader to be a pushover, but if you manage to get the balance right, you will reap the benefits in improved performance and loyalty. It is important, also, to ensure that praise is properly distributed: Make sure that you know which people have done a good piece of work and that they get positive feedback.

> Act in such a way that your humility may not be weakness, nor your authority be severity.

GREGORY THE GREAT
540–604 CE

SOURCE: *The Book of Pastoral Rule*
DATE: ca. 590
FIELD: Religion

Gregory is the only pope apart from Leo I in the 5th century to be called "the Great." He is celebrated for his learning and his writing—in addition to a 35-book study of the biblical book of Job and a collection of saints' lives, he wrote *The Book of Pastoral Rule*, a highly prized book of advice for rulers. He is traditionally also credited with standardizing the plainchant music used in church services, which is called "Gregorian chant," although modern scholars state that the music was standardized in the 8th century, more than a century after his death, by a different pope of the same name, Gregory II, who occupied the papal throne from 715 to 731.

His advice here, taken from *Pastoral Rule*, captures an important aspect of leadership: Leaders should aim to use their authority as gently as they can, but they must never be pushovers. If you feel people are disrespecting established rules, or pushing you to test your response, then you have to be strict—you cannot let people get away with cheekiness or laziness. Yet you undermine your authority if you use it indiscriminately or too harshly. The quote opposite continues, "Justice must be accompanied by humility, that humility may render justice lovable." When you use your authority, do not emphasize your power or position. As mentioned elsewhere, you do yourself no favors as a leader if you allow anger to run away with you; you can use anger, but it must be under your control. You must aim to exercise your authority in a way that is demonstrably fair to all.

Right action is better than knowledge; but in order to do what is right, we must know what is right.

CHARLES THE GREAT
748-814

SOURCE: Letter to Abbot Baugulf
DATE: ca. 780-800
FIELD: Statecraft

Charles the Great (Charlemagne), king of the Franks and first ruler of what became known as the Holy Roman Empire, was a great believer in education. At his court in Aachen he was such a committed patron of the arts and learning that the English monk Alcuin of York called the city a "new Athens," comparing it to the great city of classical Greece.

The quote opposite comes from a letter of ca. 780-800 sent by Charles to Abbot Baugulf of the Benedictine Abbey of Fulda (and probably written by Alcuin), in which the king urged the formation of schools. His particular concern was that priests and monks should learn how to read, so they could study the scriptures and gain wisdom, but he expresses a truth that has significant implications for those of us wanting to develop our leadership skills. Being a good leader is not a matter of knowledge; leaders stand or fall based on how they behave under pressure, the decisions made in the heat of the moment, the relationships they build with those they wish to inspire and lead.

Yet, just as generals study in military academies and interpret the achievements of their forerunners, so leaders can benefit from reading about great women and men who have inspired followers to action. The quote also speaks to the importance of preparation: "In order to do what is right, we must know what is right." We will benefit from carefully thinking through strategy and the rights and wrongs of a matter before we have to decide.

A LEADER CAN NEVER BE **HAPPY** UNTIL HIS PEOPLE ARE **HAPPY.**

GENGHIS KHAN
1162–1227

SOURCE: Reported saying
DATE: ca. 1225
FIELD: Military

Temujin, known to history as Genghis Khan, was a cruel warlord who founded the vast Mongol empire, which following his death became history's largest contiguous empire (one with a common border). He is an example of the importance of reputation: He was famous for the ruthlessness with which he waged war, and sometimes terrified peoples surrendered in advance. Yet once victory was assured, he set out to build an enduring peace. For example, he was committed to the shamanistic religion of the Mongols, but was happy to allow the peoples of his empire to keep their own faith, whether Muslim, Daoist, Buddhist, or Christian.

His words emphasize the importance of looking after your followers. A good leader makes sure credit and benefits are shared out. As a leader you need to make sure you know who is responsible for success, and let them know you have noticed and are pleased. Successful leaders are often those who are seen to be engaged alongside their teams, and share the hard work and difficulties that precede success. Genghis Khan himself was a leader who shared hardship—another line associated with him is, "When it was wet, we bore the wet together; when it was cold, we bore the cold together." A good leader makes sure he knows when his people are not happy. If you cannot easily work alongside your followers, then it pays to ensure you have trusted lieutenants who will report back to you on morale and general atmosphere among the workforce.

A clear and innocent conscience fears nothing.

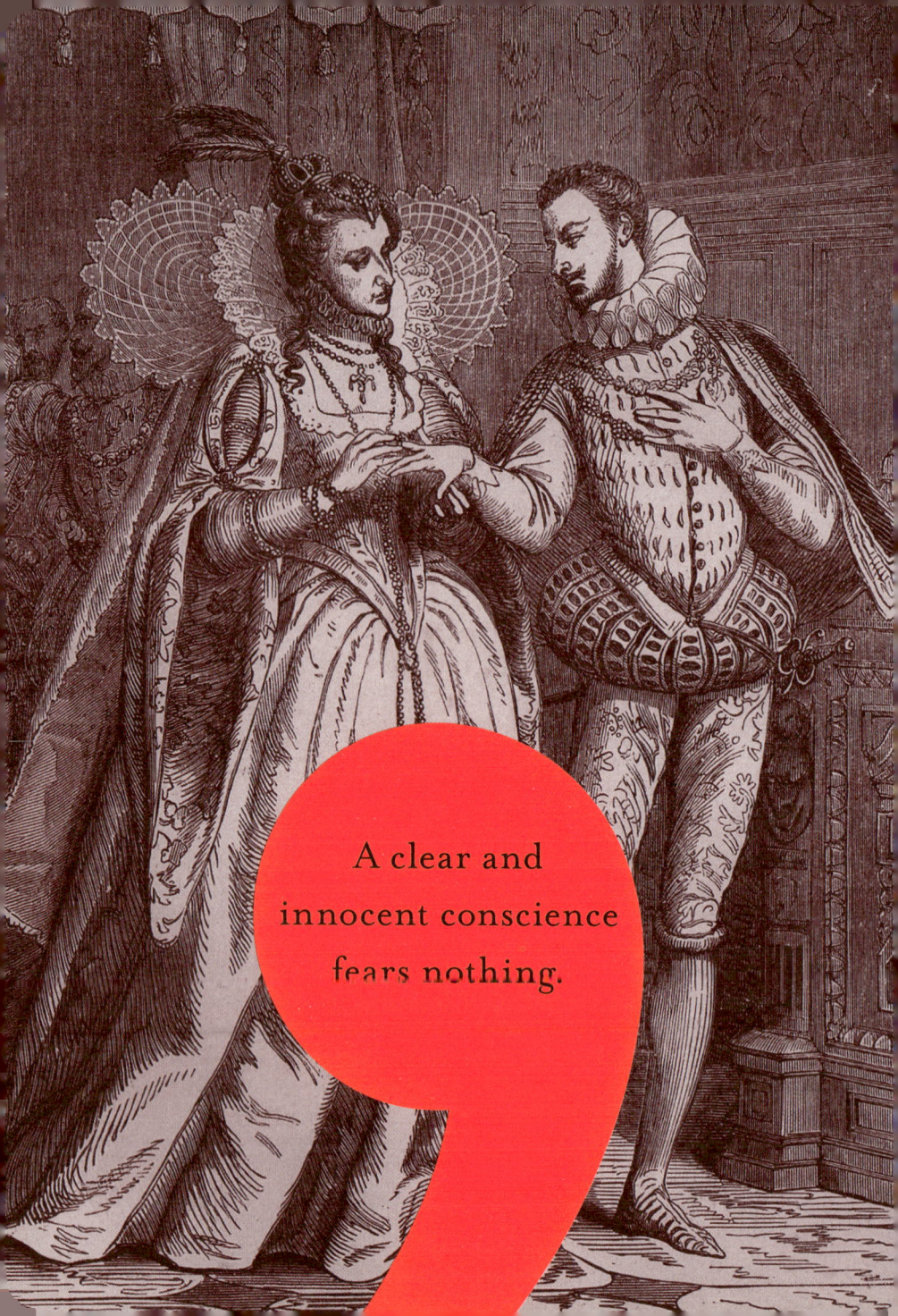

ELIZABETH I
1533–1603

SOURCE: Said to French ambassador
DATE: 1581
FIELD: Royal authority

Queen Elizabeth I of England reigned for 43 years, from 1588 to 1603, and oversaw the beginnings of the country's imperial power and a great flowering of English arts, poetry, and theater. She never married, and a carefully nurtured national mythology celebrated the idea of "the Virgin Queen," married to her people rather than a foreign prince. Close to the end of her reign in 1601, she told parliament, "Though God has raised me high, this I count the glory of my crown, that I have reigned with your loves."

The queen delivered the words opposite to the French ambassador, who had suggested she must marry his countryman, the Duke of Anjou, because there were rumors they had been physically intimate. Her words make clear the importance for leaders of not compromising themselves: Leaders should be careful of what they do, or promise, and how this may impact on later dealings. Knowing you have nothing to apologize for greatly increases your confidence. Furthermore, people who are known for being honest and fair dealing will be able to capitalize on this reputation: It will prevent gossip arising and give weight to their words, if they calmly dismiss a complaint or allegation. Arguably the words also show how powerful people can trade on their position, if not their reputation.

In the quote, Elizabeth is effectively saying, "Rumors may come and go; it is enough that I say they are not true." Leaders may be able to cover over minor difficulties, if their authority is secure.

Knowledge itself is power.

SIR FRANCIS BACON
1561–1626

SOURCE: *Sacred Meditations*
DATE: 1597
FIELDS: Philosophy/statecraft

Sir Francis Bacon was a British lawyer who served as Lord Chancellor under King James I between 1618 and 1621, and was also a profound thinker, celebrated for his essays. He was the first writer in England to use the essay form and was so powerful a creative thinker that in the 19th century some people began to argue that he was the true author of the plays attributed to William Shakespeare. Major figures, including Mark Twain, Friedrich Nietzsche, and mathematician Georg Cantor were convinced, but the theory is today largely discredited.

The words opposite are taken from his work *Sacred Meditations*, published in 1597, and in context refer to God's knowledge. They come from a section in which Bacon is distinguishing between God's power as expressed in His knowledge and God's power as expressed in His actions. Knowing is different from doing; having knowledge does not bring results on its own. However, knowing things puts you in a position to act more effectively. The power of knowledge is clear, if you consider a situation in which you know something your rival does not – perhaps you are competing for a contract and you have inside knowledge about the client's future plans.

As a leader, "knowledge" may mean knowing and understanding theories of management and leadership; it may mean really understanding the field in which you operate; it may mean knowing your followers and what drives and inspires them. It may also mean understanding yourself: What do you need to operate at your best?

Our doubts are traitors and make us lose the good we oft might win, by fearing to attempt.

WILLIAM SHAKESPEARE
1564–1616

SOURCE: *Measure for Measure*
DATE: ca. 1603
FIELD: Theater

English playwright, poet, and actor William Shakespeare is celebrated as the world's greatest dramatist. He wrote at least 37 plays from 1588 on, including the world-famous *Hamlet* and *Romeo and Juliet*, as well as his beautiful sonnets and other poems, including *Venus and Adonis* (1593). The line opposite comes from his play *Measure for Measure*, written ca. 1603, and is spoken by Lucio, who is urging Isabella to act to save the life of her brother Claudio, who has been sentenced to death. He is urging her to go to Angelo, who has delivered the death sentence, to kneel and beg for Claudio's life, and when she doubts she can make a difference, he tells her, "Our doubts are traitors...."

Like anyone else, leaders can be prone to doubt. Sometimes rethinking a decision can be beneficial and can save us from a mistake, but often doubts undermine our effectiveness. This is particularly true of self-doubt, which is what Lucio is arguing against. If we doubt our ability, we may opt out of a challenge, and, as Lucio says, not attempting to win is the surest way to lose. Leaders in particular need to model self-confidence. It is a key quality, to show they believe in a project and in the means of achieving it. Doubts are traitors, Lucio says: They are actively working against us, like a double agent. It is not good to ignore traitors or doubts; we need to identify them, interrogate them, and put them in their place.

The shortest answer is doing.

GEORGE HERBERT
1593–1633

SOURCE: *Jacula Prudentum*
DATE: 1652
FIELD: Poetry

George Herbert was a poet and priest. After graduating from Cambridge University he was a member of parliament from 1624 until 1625, during the reign of King James I, and then settled down as a Church of England rector of St. Andrew's in Lower Bemerton near Salisbury in western England. He was a very fine poet, and is often connected to the group of "metaphysical poets," including the more famous John Donne and Andrew Marvell. Herbert was also a collector of English proverbs, publishing *Outlandish Proverbs* in 1640 and *Jacula Prudentum* in 1652. The phrase opposite, from the second of these books, is one of these proverbs.

The lesson for leaders is that you can think and think about a problem, but the swiftest remedy is to take action. Of course there is a danger in being hasty, and it is often necessary to think things through carefully. Yet, as we all know, you can get bogged down in thinking and forget that, for all the thinking you may do, usually it is the action that really matters. This proverb is intended as a piece of corrective advice—imagine it being delivered to someone who has been talking for a long time about a whole series of options. Do not forget, it seems to be saying, you may be best off doing something rather than agonizing over it. You can always act again, if necessary, to put things right. Other quotes collected in the book caution against the dangers of diving in too quickly. The wisdom leaders need is knowing when to stop and when to go.

Soldiers' bellies are not satisfied with empty promises and hopes.

PETER THE GREAT
1672–1725

SOURCE: Reported saying
DATE: ca. 1715
FIELD: Generalship

Peter was an autocratic ruler who transformed Russia through a series of modernizing reforms. He liked to be hands-on and mix with the people; he worked incognito as a carpenter while gaining experience to back up his modernizing program, and in St. Petersburg, the new capital he founded, he would dress in an old soldier's uniform and drink beer with sailors and shipbuilders. He went face-to-face with his subjects and gained an understanding of what life was like for people at the bottom of the pile.

So he knew what he was talking about when he made the comment opposite. Leaders should aim to give their followers what they need, rather than fine words and sweeping rhetoric. They have to deliver. In order to do this, they have to understand what their followers' needs are. If soldiers are hungry, they need food; when people are really struggling to make ends meet, they need a bonus or a pay rise and not an inspirational talk.

Sometimes leaders can get cut off from reality, to a certain extent. They may be cushioned by their conditions of work and financial package and forget how challenging things can be for some of the people they are leading. Or the leaders may simply never have experienced how difficult it is, say, for a single parent to cope with a full-time job, school events, and childcare costs. It is important to make every effort to "get real" when thinking about placing demands on team members, say, or devising benefits or rewards.

Judge a man by his questions rather than his answers.

VOLTAIRE
1694–1778

SOURCE: Reported statement
DATE: ca. 1750
FIELD: Philosophy

Voltaire was the pen name of François-Marie Arouet, French Enlightenment philosopher, historian, poet, and prose writer. He was a staunch advocate of freedom of religion and of speech who published *Candide* (1759) and *A Philosophical Dictionary* (1764), a kind of encyclopedia. After a clash with the Duke of Orléans, he was thrown in the Bastille prison in 1717 then exiled to England from 1726 until 1729. He asked difficult questions in order to probe beliefs and accepted knowledge from unusual positions.

It is an important insight that the quality of what you find out depends on the caliber of the questions you ask. When you are a leader, it is well to remember that just because questions are being asked and checks are in place, that does not necessarily mean all is well. We all need to consider whether we are checking the right things and asking the right questions. It is also a necessary step to try to reconsider the assumptions that shape how you think about your work, your institution, or the people you lead. Sometimes the questions you need to ask may not even occur to you because of your background, sex, race, and experience, so it is vital to get others' input.

It is also true, as Voltaire's words imply, that you can get great insight into how able people are or how acutely they understand an issue by listening to the questions they ask. When you are judging team members or appraising people's work, you will be able to get valuable insights from the questions they bring to the discussion.

He who defends everything defends nothing.

FREDERICK THE GREAT
1712–1786

SOURCE: Reported saying
DATE: ca. 1760
FIELD: Military tactics

Frederick the Great was a brilliant general who made Prussia a major force in Europe. As a leader he placed great emphasis on discipline and duty and said a prince was the "soul of a state." He was a hands-on general who shared the hardships of his followers on campaign and often led his troops into battle. Frederick said wars should be "short and fought quickly" and often took significant risks in order to strike a decisive blow with his mobile, highly disciplined troops. He was greatly admired by no less a figure than Napoleon Bonaparte of France, who studied his military tactics and visited his tomb in Potsdam in 1807.

Frederick's words are an observation on military tactics that is applicable in many fields. In the military context, if you have, say, a long border to defend and a limited number of troops, you will be overrun if you try to string the troops out to defend the entire border. Instead, you have to pick the most strategic spots to defend and then defend them in force. The same idea is valuable more generally in leadership. It is an important skill to be able to pinpoint likely threats, identify weak spots, and concentrate your resources there. The insight is often quoted by IT gurus in companies, who say that you cannot defend a network or company IT system against every possible threat on the Internet. Your task is to identify the most likely threats and your own weak spots and then put strong defenses in place.

We ought not to look back,
unless it is to derive useful
lessons from past errors.

GEORGE WASHINGTON
1732–1799

SOURCE: Letter to John Armstrong
DATE: March 26, 1781
FIELD: American presidency

Commander in Chief of the Continental Army in the American Revolutionary War and first US president, George Washington was hailed by his contemporaries as the "father of the country" and is celebrated today as a leadership role model for all. A physically imposing man and a courageous, inspirational military leader, he had a strong sense of duty, led by example, and did all he could to bring about unity in the fledgling United States. He wrote the words shown opposite on March 26, 1781, to his friend John Armstrong, whom he had met during a military campaign against Fort Duquesne (near modern-day Pittsburgh, Pennsylvania) in 1758, when Washington was commanding a contingent of Virginians in the British Army.

Washington's words are very useful advice to leaders. There is little point in looking back at what you or your followers have done, except to determine what you can learn from past mistakes to improve how you perform in the future. We may prefer not to consider past setbacks, but looking back at them is worthwhile, and it generates useful questions, such as: "What can we do differently next time?" "Do any of the circumstances that impacted then still apply?" There may be occasions when it is useful to look at past successes, perhaps to build personal or group morale, or to consider which aspects of past victories can be repeated. There is, however, the danger of becoming complacent, and often circumstances have changed and the process may only distract you from looking forward and engaging with the next challenge.

> Treat people as if they were what they ought to be, and you help them become what they are capable of being.

JOHANN WOLFGANG VON GOETHE
1749-1832

SOURCE: *Wilhelm Meister's Apprenticeship*
DATE: 1795-1796
FIELD: Literature

Romantic poet, playwright, and novelist Johann Wolfgang von Goethe is probably the greatest of all German writers. He is famous for such works as the novel *The Sorrows of Young Werther* (1774) and his verse-drama *Faust*, published in two parts in 1808 and 1832, a version of the legend of the medieval German doctor who sold his soul to the devil in return for magical powers and occult knowledge. Goethe was also an accomplished scientist who wrote a treatise on the theory of light in 1810.

The quote shown opposite is a version of a line from his second novel, *Wilhelm Meister's Apprenticeship*, published in four volumes in 1795–1796. In its fuller form, the quote suggests that you make people worse if you take them "as they are." When you treat people "as if they were what they should be," you improve them. The idea is widely discussed on leadership forums because it delivers an intriguing and powerful insight into managing and developing team members and subordinate colleagues. It might be paraphrased as, "If you are forever checking on people, they will behave as if they need to be monitored." If you trust people, however, they will become trustworthy. If you have lots of rules, people will find ways to break them.

There is risk attached to this approach, of course, but the trust method can be powerfully effective. Demonstrate to people that you are relying on them to be self-managing, and they may regulate their work better.

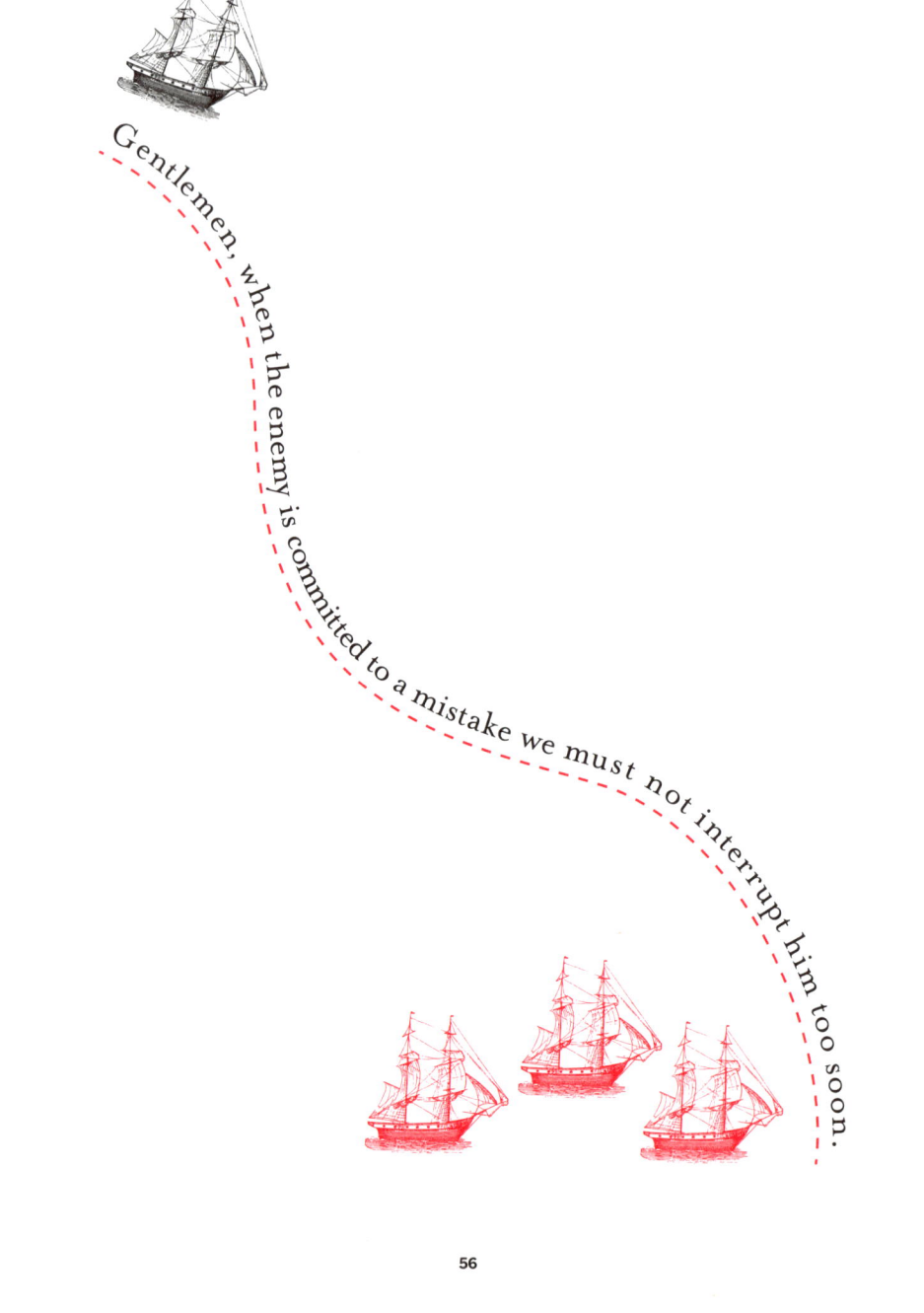

Gentlemen, when the enemy is committed to a mistake we must not interrupt him too soon.

HORATIO, LORD NELSON
1758–1805

SOURCE: Reported saying
DATE: ca. 1800
FIELD: Naval tactics

Today a statue of this British naval hero stands on top of Nelson's Column in Trafalgar Square, central London. The column was erected in 1840–43 to commemorate the life and heroic leadership of Nelson, who died on October 21, 1805, while leading the Royal Navy to victory over the French and Spanish navies at the Battle of Trafalgar. Before the battle, one of the greatest naval victories in British history, he famously sent a signal to the fleet, "England expects that every man will do his duty." Like many leaders in this book, he had a strong sense of duty himself, and was also celebrated for his inspiring leadership and his tactical and strategic skill.

The quote opposite delivers the valuable insight that sometimes leadership involves standing back and letting events unfold. If your rival or enemy is making a mistake, the best thing you can do as a leader is prepare yourself and your team, so you are ready to benefit from it. In Nelson's case this would have involved sitting tight and waiting for the enemy to move into a position that made his fleet vulnerable. The worst thing you can do is make an intervention that might alert the rival that they are going wrong or might dissipate your advantage in some other way. Of course, we need to take note of the "too soon" at the end: As leaders, we will interrupt our rivals, but only when the moment is right to accrue maximum advantage.

A leader is a dealer in hope.

NAPOLEON BONAPARTE
1769-1821

SOURCE: Reported saying
DATE: ca. 1815
FIELD: Generalship

Strong-willed and powerfully ambitious, Napoleon Bonaparte rose from humble beginnings to become emperor of France, and he transformed Europe as he carried the country to greatness. He was a tactical genius, bold and decisive in battle, and a magnificent leader who established a powerful rapport with his troops. He would wander through the army camp and talk to his men around the campfires; they loved the man they nicknamed "the Little Corporal," on account of his short stature, and would do anything for him. As a leader he used his self-confidence, optimism, and hope as tools to drive his followers to success. Yet he also proved himself again and again in battle, so it was clear his self-confidence was well founded.

When a leader is dealing in hope, she convinces people of her vision—that goals can be achieved, targets hit, and that things get better. Hope and success become matters of collective belief, such as when Barack Obama and his audiences declared together when he was campaigning to become US president in 2008, "Yes we can!" A dealer in hope carries people with him and enables them to perform to the peak of their ability. Napoleon declared, "The moral is to the physical as three to one," meaning that self-belief and mental strength are three times as important as physical force. In this context the leader herself may become essential to achievement because she inspires people by her very presence. According to the Duke of Wellington, Napoleon's presence on the battlefield was worth 40,000 soldiers—he inspired his followers to greatness.

I cannot trust a man
to control others
who cannot
c o n t r o l
himself.

ROBERT E. LEE
1807–1870

SOURCE: Reported saying
DATE: ca. 1865
FIELD: Generalship

Robert E. Lee was a leading general of the Confederate Army in the American Civil War. One of the best military officers in the US, he had been offered command of the Union Army by President Lincoln, but as a native of Virginia chose to serve the South as military adviser to the president of the Confederacy, commander of the army of Northern Virginia, and finally general in chief of the Confederate armies. He had a strong sense of duty and stressed the importance of self-control—he famously said of whiskey, "I like it; I always have; and that's the reason I never use it."

To control and direct others, Lee says, you need authority, and your authority suffers when you lose control. Schoolchildren, for example, will lose respect for a teacher if they see her out of control. Leaders need to be able to demonstrate self-control. If your colleagues, team members, or staff see you overwhelmed by anxiety, say, or flailing around in anger, you will need to act later to put things right. If you feel your self-control threatened, it is well to absent yourself from a meeting or public space; it can be helpful to take a brisk walk or sit quietly someplace private and try to breathe deeply and slowly for a few minutes. Disputes can escalate quickly and unpredictably, if those involved are out of control and wild things are said. If you model self-control, you can expect it in others. Then your dealings with your colleagues and followers can be measured and courteous.

The best way to destroy an enemy

is to make him a friend.

ABRAHAM LINCOLN
1809–1865

SOURCE: Reported saying in US Civil War
DATE: ca. 1865
FIELD: American presidency

Abraham Lincoln is often cited as the greatest of all US presidents. A superb communicator and negotiator, he abolished slavery in the United States and carried the country through the trauma of the Civil War. He had the capacity to make a straightforward connection with those he spoke to—they called him "Honest Abe"—and the gift of winning over former antagonists and embedding them into his program, as he did with William H. Seward, his rival for the Republican nomination for the presidency in 1860, whom the following year Lincoln made Secretary of State. Seward became one of Lincoln's closest allies.

An ability to win opponents over makes for a very special—and highly effective—leader. People who are able to do this treat their enemies with respect and take the other side's position seriously. If you and a colleague or subordinate disagree about a problem, try to view the problem, not the other person, as your enemy. That way, you and the other become allies in trying to find a solution to the difficulty. It is not such a large step, then, for the person to come over to your side. Lincoln was noted for using humor, and leaders often benefit from having a good-natured sense of fun. Of course, jokes must not be mean spirited, leaders should laugh with people, not at them. The key is not to lose sight of the fact that your antagonist is a rounded human being, little different from you yourself.

Doing is the great thing. For if, resolutely, people do what is right, in time they will come to like doing it.

JOHN RUSKIN
1819-1900

SOURCE: From the lecture "Traffic"
DATE: 1866
FIELD: The arts

Victorian art critic John Ruskin is best known for his five-volume *Modern Painters* (1843–60), which he began to defend the artist J. M. W. Turner, and for his books praising the medieval Gothic style in architecture. Ruskin also wrote and lectured about culture and society.

The quote comes from his lecture "Traffic," delivered in Bradford Town Hall, in northern England, in 1866. The line comes from a passage in which Ruskin argues that it is more important to *do* the right thing than to *want* to do the right thing—a man may want to spend all day drinking wine, but so long as he keeps away from alcohol and stays sober he is doing the right thing. Yet Ruskin goes on to say that the man is only in "a right moral state" if he comes to like being sober—it is not good to be longing all the time to drink wine, even if he is staying sober with gritted teeth.

His key point is that doing the right thing makes you come to enjoy doing the right thing: "In time, they will come to like doing it." There are many applications for leaders. For one, good practice reinforces itself. You get into good habits, and you come to like the good habits you have. As a leader you can model good ways of working and interacting with colleagues and subordinates. You can seek to create a workplace culture in which people want to be industrious and creative, and to show one another respect and courtesy.

Keep your fears to yourself, but share your courage with others.

ROBERT LOUIS STEVENSON
1850-1894

SOURCE: Reported saying
DATE: ca. 1890
FIELD: Literature

In *Treasure Island* and *Strange Case of Dr. Jekyll and Mr. Hyde*, Scottish author Robert Louis Stevenson wrote two of the most famous books of the late 19th century. Born in Edinburgh, he was driven by poor health to live much of his life abroad, and he wrote many excellent travel books before settling at last on Samoa in the South Seas. In the course of his life he demonstrated a forthright courage in coping with his poor health and in standing up to his father's disapproval when he became involved with a married American woman, Fanny Vandegrift Osbourne, whom he finally married.

The quote opposite is a favorite on leadership blogs. It is true that as a leader there is nothing to be gained from making your doubts and fears public. This is not to say that you should not recognize what disturbs you; it is a good thing to be willing to discuss it in private with a confidant and develop coping strategies. With colleagues more generally, however, the leader should aim to share and model—strength of mind and purpose, qualities that enable you to be even-handed and positive. Perhaps the quality Stevenson is calling on is the courage to remain unruffled he wrote in praise of not allowing yourself to be swept up by good fortune or dragged down by bad, when he noted that, "Quiet minds cannot be perplexed or frightened but go on in fortune or misfortune at their own private pace, like a clock during a thunderstorm."

> We are not interested in the possibilities of defeat; they do not exist.

QUEEN VICTORIA
1819–1901

SOURCE: Statement to British statesman Arthur Balfour
DATE: December 1899
FIELD: Monarchical rule

Queen Victoria gave her name to the Victorian Age, during which the British Empire—the largest the world has ever seen—reached its zenith. Coming to the throne in 1837, at a time when the reputation of the monarchy had been damaged by the excesses of the early kings of the House of Hanover, and only partially repaired by her uncle William IV, she stabilized the institution, bringing security, dutiful service, and a strong will. She reigned for more than 60 years until her death in 1901, aged 81. As a leader she was energetic, courageous, forthright, and dogged. The British Empire was not interested in the possibility of defeat: it grew to cover 12.7 million square miles (32.9 million sq km) and contain 444 million people.

Sometimes self-belief and strength of will are what is needed in a leader. In the face of a setback or a major challenge that requires people to pull together, indomitable determination of the kind demonstrated by Victoria's words will inspire followers. If, like Victoria, a leader refuses to recognize that failure is possible, then there will be no giving up. Of course, there is no benefit in being blindly optimistic and refusing to recognize problems—unless a leader is extraordinarily charismatic, followers will not troop loyally after him to their doom. Self-belief in a leader needs to be allied to achievement, planning, and strategic intelligence. Yet a refusal to give up, a determination to find a way to make things happen—these can inspire people to defy difficulty and achieve success against all odds.

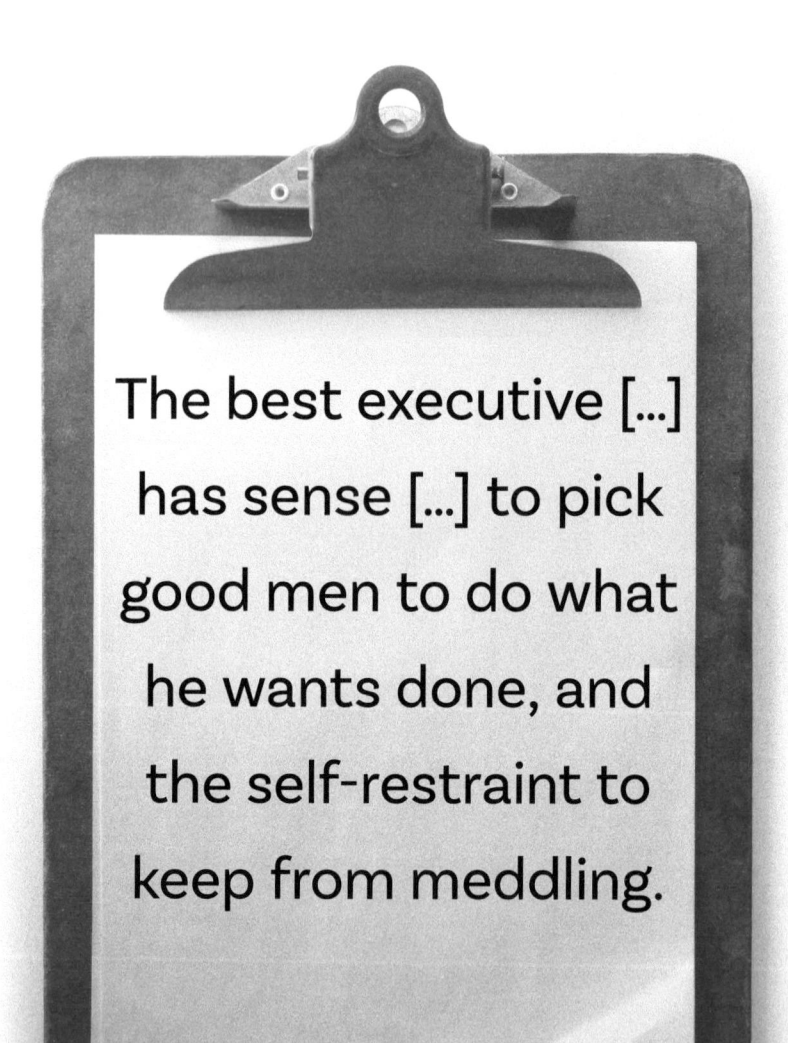

The best executive [...] has sense [...] to pick good men to do what he wants done, and the self-restraint to keep from meddling.

THEODORE ROOSEVELT
1858–1918

SOURCE: Attributed
DATE: ca. 1905
FIELD: American presidency

The flamboyant Teddy Roosevelt thrust himself into public consciousness when he led a volunteer cavalry troop known as "Roosevelt's Rough Riders" in Cuba during the Spanish–American War of 1898. Subsequently he was governor of New York from 1898 until 1900, then vice-president. When President McKinley was assassinated in September 1901, Roosevelt became president and then won election for another term in 1904. He was a reformer in domestic politics and active overseas. He won the 1906 Nobel Peace Prize for his efforts to mediate in the Russo-Japanese War of 1904–05 and exercised US authority over settling the route and construction of the Panama Canal.

The words opposite are another reminder that leaders cannot do it all. It is not just that we do not have enough energy or time to do everything. It is also the case that people in a team or organization will find it dispiriting and disempowering if they feel you do not trust them. As the quote suggests, delegation is a key leadership skill and has two important aspects: first, choosing well, and second, stepping back and allowing people to get on with the task you have entrusted to them. What is more, an executive who genuinely chooses well in this area will pick people who, in order to thrive, need to take the initiative and be free to make decisions for themselves. The best people will not accept being constantly supervised or having to seek permission and sign-offs all the time. The best people are themselves leaders, and the leader's role involves allowing them to develop.

One person with passion is better than forty people merely interested.

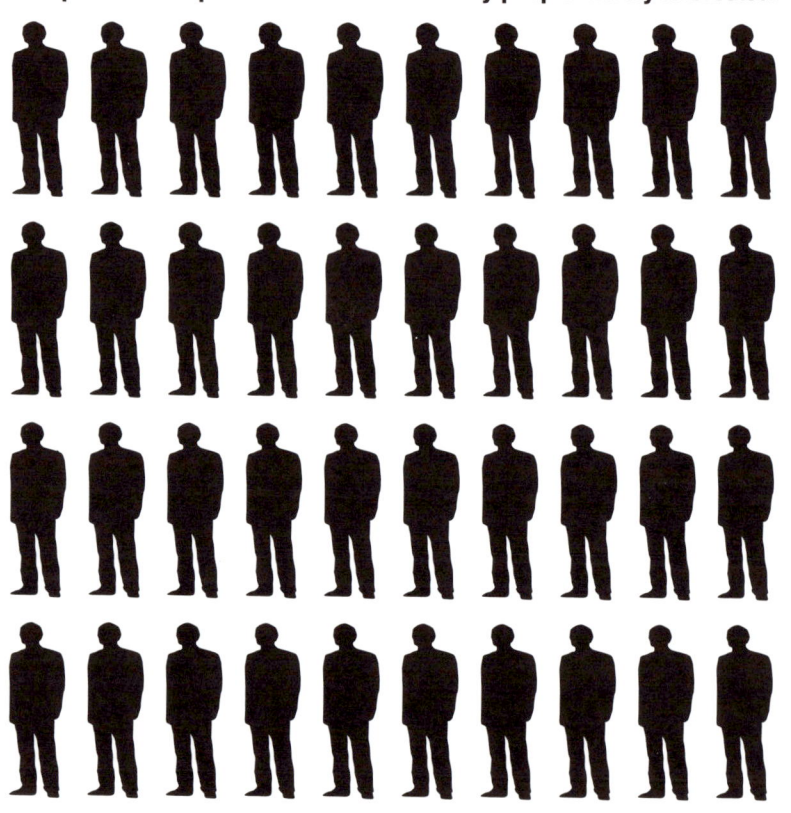

E. M. FORSTER
1879–1970

SOURCE: Reported saying
DATE: ca. 1910
FIELD: Literature

British novelist and critic E. M. Forster is celebrated for his novels *Howards End* and *A Passage to India*. He urged people to be truthful and make human connections at a time when he felt that social change was making this harder. His famous phrase "Only connect" was the epigraph to *Howards End*, published in 1910. In a famous passage from the novel, he distinguished between prose, meaning everyday reality, and passion, meaning excitement and engagement with life; the words "Only connect" were the "sermon" of the character Margaret Schlegel, an idealistic young woman who thought people need to connect the "prose and the passion" and "live in fragments no longer."

The person with passion referred to in Forster's words opposite is someone who is not going through the motions but is fully engaged and alive. This person is like a singer or poet compared to the "merely interested" person, who is like the writer of a report; you need reports, you need prose, but you also need the rare qualities of the engaged person, who has drive and takes joy in a task. The passionate person has the unstoppable quality, the refusal to give up that we have identified as a key leadership trait; she is also alive to possibility, so creative in finding solutions to problems and new ways of doing things, and showing others the way.

This kind of energy is contagious—a leader with passion is an inspirational figure who models the way to drive a company, department, or project forward. The passion will spread from the one leader to the forty followers.

Be militant each in your own way [...] I incite this meeting to rebellion.

EMMELINE PANKHURST
1858–1928

SOURCE: Speech at the Royal Albert Hall, London
DATE: October 17, 1912
FIELD: Suffragism

Emmeline Pankhurst, British leader of the campaign for women to have an equal right to vote in elections, delivered these stirring words in a speech at the Royal Albert Hall, London, on October 17, 1912. It was her first speech after being released from prison, where she had been sent after being convicted of "conspiracy to commit property damage." The bruising women's suffrage campaign, which involved a great deal of suffering for many women who took part in hunger strikes and suffered forced-feeding interventions in prison, finally achieved its goal when women were granted the same voting rights as men in 1928. Success came just a few weeks before Emmeline Pankhurst's death on June 14 that year.

Militancy may seem a dangerous thing for leaders to urge on their followers. Here it represents the power of commitment and refusal to give way to an unjust repression. Pankhurst represented her followers and their cause as unstoppable. She was the kind of leader who modeled behavior her followers could copy, fearlessly taking on the authorities and being repeatedly arrested and imprisoned. She also called on her listeners to be militant because being resistant and troublesome, standing up for their rights, was the kind of behavior that women had been conditioned to avoid. As a leader you almost certainly will not urge your followers to break the law, but you may well find yourself urging them to bring total commitment to the task at hand, to get away from conditioned behavior and get out of their comfort zone.

You are here to enrich the world.

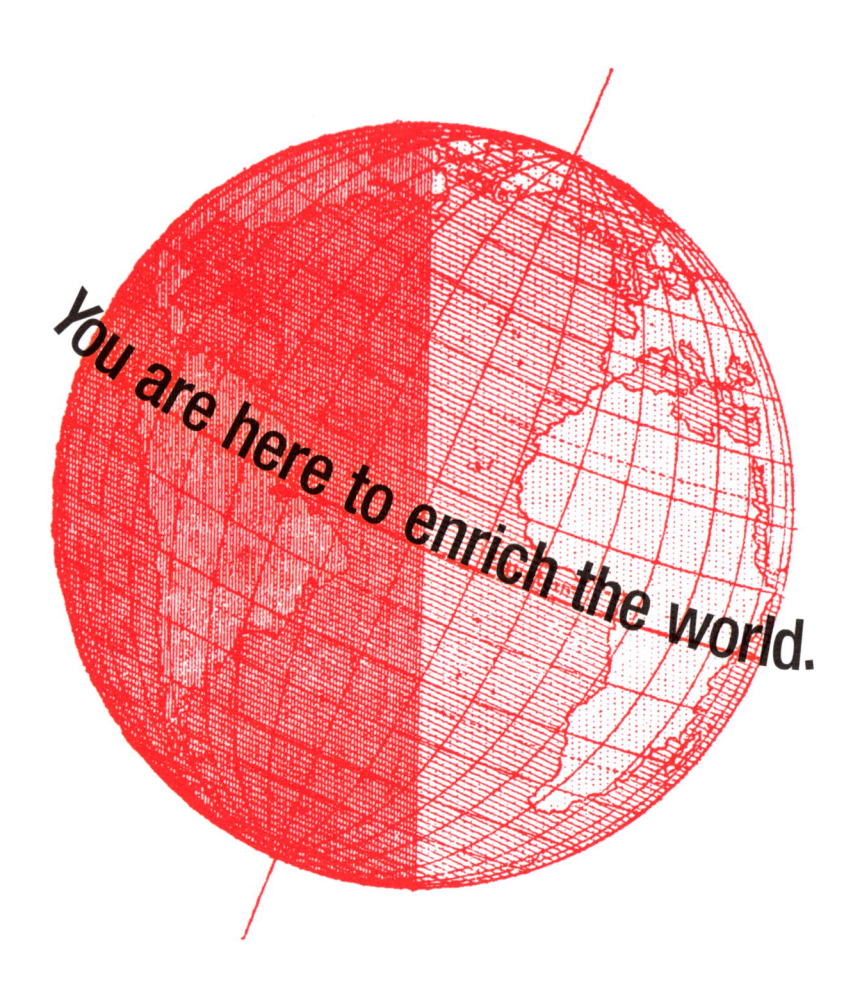

WOODROW WILSON
1856–1921

SOURCE: Speech at Swarthmore College, Swarthmore, Pennsylvania
DATE: October 25, 1913
FIELD: American presidency

Woodrow Wilson, 28th president of the United States, led his country into the First World War and afterward played a central role in the creation of the League of Nations—for which he was awarded the Nobel Peace Prize in 1919. He delivered the advice opposite when speaking at Swarthmore College on October 25, 1913. It comes from a passage in which he urged his listeners to commit to serving humanity: "Do you covet distinction? You will get it only as the servant of mankind […] You are not here merely to prepare to make a living […] You are here to enrich the world, and you impoverish yourself if you forget the errand."

President Wilson's approach was to attempt to draw out the best in his listeners. It will be of great benefit to you as a leader if you develop the ability to make a human connection—to call on your people's deepest resources, their inner strength. Then you can harness their highest drives or ambitions. If you can say that your endeavor is not about earning money or winning prestige, but about making a change for the better, about serving and "enriching the world," as Wilson characterizes the students' calling, then you will engage new levels of drive, energy, and commitment. This connection with a leader will enable followers to make the most of themselves; people love a leader who encourages them not to settle for less but to aim for more. As President Wilson said, "you impoverish yourself" if you do not remember what your better self calls on you to do.

> Learn to know every man under you, get under his skin […] Then cater to him—with kindness or roughness as his case may demand.

JOHN McGRAW
1873–1934

SOURCE: Quoted in *Literary Digest*
DATE: 1914
FIELD: Sports

John McGraw is recognized as one of the greatest sports managers of all time. He inspired the New York Giants baseball team to ten National League championships while their coach between 1902 and 1932, including a run of four successive wins between 1921 and 1924. Previously he had been a top player for the Baltimore Orioles. Tough, uncompromising, brave, and single-minded, he was a winner above all. As manager he was famous for picking up players others had discarded and breathing new life into their careers. He knew everything about man-management.

He advises leaders to really get to know their people. If you really know what makes people tick, you can tailor your treatment of them precisely to meet their needs. Some people need a firm hand—they may find it difficult to get going or like to challenge authority. Sometimes a fierce, demanding approach really inspires people to perform. Your approval is hard to win, and they work hard to win it. Others need an arm around their shoulders; they need supportive advice, or practical help, and understanding; you may sometimes need to relax rules to enable them to flourish.

McGraw was a disciplinarian who ruled partly through fear. It is important to note that your authority needs to be secure if you are going to manage people in this way, with different approaches for different people. Yet this kind of leadership can be really inspirational and reap great results. Super-successful rival coach Connie Mack said, "There has only been one manager—and his name is McGraw."

No man will make a great leader who wants to do it all himself, or to get all the credit for doing it.

ANDREW CARNEGIE
1835–1919

SOURCE: Reported saying
DATE: ca. 1915
FIELD: Industry

Scottish-born American industrialist Andrew Carnegie made a vast fortune in the expansion of the American steel industry during the late 19th century and then in 1901 became a great philanthropist, distributing some $350 million to good causes in the US and the British Empire. He embodies the American dream, rising from a penniless immigrant from Dunfermline, Scotland, who began work aged 13 as a bobbin boy in a textile mill in what is now Pittsburgh, Pennsylvania, to become the world's richest man. Yet he shared the product of his hard work—he saw the redistribution of wealth as a profoundly important duty and wrote that a "man who dies rich dies disgraced."

His comment warns bosses against trying to "do it all." Leaders need to be able to choose able associates and delegate tasks effectively. Sometimes it takes courage to let go. You may have worked tirelessly for a long time developing a project or enterprise, but if it is to succeed there usually will come a time when you have to share it. Equally, Carnegie says, leaders should not feel the need to get all the glory. Letting go may involve allowing others to take some of the credit for the achievement you dream of. For there is certainly a selfless aspect to good leadership—key skills are finding and developing good colleagues to assist you and drawing out subordinates' confidence and skills as you enable them to succeed. A leader's focus needs to be on the enterprise and not on him- or herself.

A teacher can never truly teach unless he is still learning himself.

" 39

RABINDRANATH TAGORE
1861–1941

SOURCE: From the essay "An Eastern University"
DATE: 1921
FIELD: Arts and teaching

Bengali poet and philosopher Rabindranath Tagore was the first author from Asia to win the Nobel Prize for Literature. He was also an educator and in 1901 in rural Bengal founded Shantiniketan ("Place of Peace"), the first school to combine Eastern and Western educational approaches and philosophy. He was a man of many talents who wrote essays, plays, novels, and short stories and traveled widely, lecturing in the West. He certainly stayed open to new challenges; he took up fine art in his 60s and became one of India's foremost painters.

Leaders need to be alive to their work. We probably all have memories of schoolteachers going through the motions while teaching a subject they had taught over and over for many years and of how boring their classes were—not because they were doing anything wrong, but because they were bored themselves; they had lost their passion. Tagore says teachers need to keep learning to make sure they are alive to their subject; as leaders we need to look for ways to keep sharp and engaged. Perhaps we need to delegate part of our current workload and take on a new and unfamiliar role in the process? Maybe we should look at professional development?

We are most successful when we are engaged, and the work is full of meaning for us and still challenges us to do more or do better. Then we can engage actively and creatively with our colleagues, in the give and take of making things happen.

Sincerity is the surest road to confidence.

DAVID LLOYD GEORGE
1863–1945

SOURCE: Speech in Aberystwyth, Wales
DATE: August 3, 1928
FIELD: Politics

British politician David Lloyd George was celebrated for his eloquence, creativity, hard work, and radical approach. Some historians place him second only to Winston Churchill among British prime ministers of the 20th century. As prime minister from 1916 his energetic leadership during the latter stage of the First World War gained him the accolade "the man who won the war," then in 1918 he achieved a landslide election victory after declaring his intention to make his country "a land fit for heroes to live in." He laid the foundations of the British welfare state, creating the country's first unemployment protection and national insurance schemes. He delivered the line opposite in a speech in Aberystwyth, Wales, on August 3, 1928.

His advice suggests that speaking honestly as a leader makes you more convincing, to other people and to yourself. If you are arguing a point you truly believe in, you will not be undermined by self-doubt. Other people are more likely to trust you if they judge you to be sincere. One implication is that when you have to deliver bad news it is best to do it straightforwardly. Say you have to ask your team to redo a task, give up a benefit, or go the extra mile, win their trust by presenting the difficult news in an open way. Another aspect of this issue is that being honest with yourself about what your feelings and ambitions are will make you a more convincing operator. Do not undermine yourself; follow a straight line.

Don't find fault;
find a remedy.

HENRY FORD
1863–1947

SOURCE: Reported saying
DATE: Not known
FIELD: Industry

The founder in 1903 of the Ford Motor Company, Henry Ford became one of the world's richest men after pioneering assembly-line factory work and selling 15.5 million Ford Model Ts, the first motor car that Americans of ordinary means could afford. The system of mass production and consumption he pioneered is named "Fordism" after him. Ford was a man of contradictions: he yearned for the farming society he had known near Dearborn, Michigan, despite deriving his wealth and position from the motor industry that helped to sweep it away. He paid his workers a good minimum wage of $5 a day in 1914 (more than double the industry average) and limited working hours, but was fiercely authoritarian in dealing with his workforce and used company police to fight unionization.

Ford was celebrated for being curious and practical, qualities reflected in the quote opposite. When things go wrong, the best leaders focus not on assigning blame so much as finding a solution. If you have to give feedback on unsatisfactory work, for example, Ford's very good advice is to focus on ways in which your colleagues can improve their performance. As much as possible, put what has gone wrong to one side and try to agree a way forward. If you are correcting work, do not just mark mistakes; instead, suggest improvements. In managing your career, similarly, do not beat yourself up when things go wrong—look for new approaches to try, new paths to follow. How can I do better? What is the next step? This positive approach keeps you improving.

> The task of leadership is not to put greatness into humanity, but to elicit it, for the greatness is there already.

JOHN BUCHAN
1875–1940

SOURCE: The lecture "Montrose on Leadership"
DATE: 1930
FIELD: Literature

Scottish novelist and diplomat John Buchan wrote *The Thirty-Nine Steps*, famously filmed by Alfred Hitchcock in 1935. He was a member of parliament, a journalist for *The Times*, a private secretary in the diplomatic service, and the government's Director of Information in the First World War. He ended his career as Governor General of Canada from 1935 until 1940. He delivered the statement opposite in a lecture, "Montrose on Leadership," published in 1930.

This advice chimes with the insight we have discussed elsewhere in this book, that a leader's role is to draw out the best in people, so enabling them to make the most of themselves. If you are a good leader you believe in your colleagues and team-members, and show them you believe in them. You give them confidence to try new tasks, to suggest creative ideas. You convince them that their efforts and creativity will be noticed and appreciated. Buchan's insight should also give a leader confidence in her team-members and colleagues: these people have all the abilities you need and your task is to help them grow to their full stature. Working with them, giving positive feedback, seeking to find remedies rather than faults (see page 86), you make them feel unstoppable; you convince them that it is only a matter of time before they make their own success. Compare the insights from Nelson Mandela (see page 147) that the best "lead from behind and put others in front" and from the *Daodejing* (see page 9) that a good leader takes followers to a position whereby they can say of a success, "We did it ourselves."

When people talk, listen **completely.**

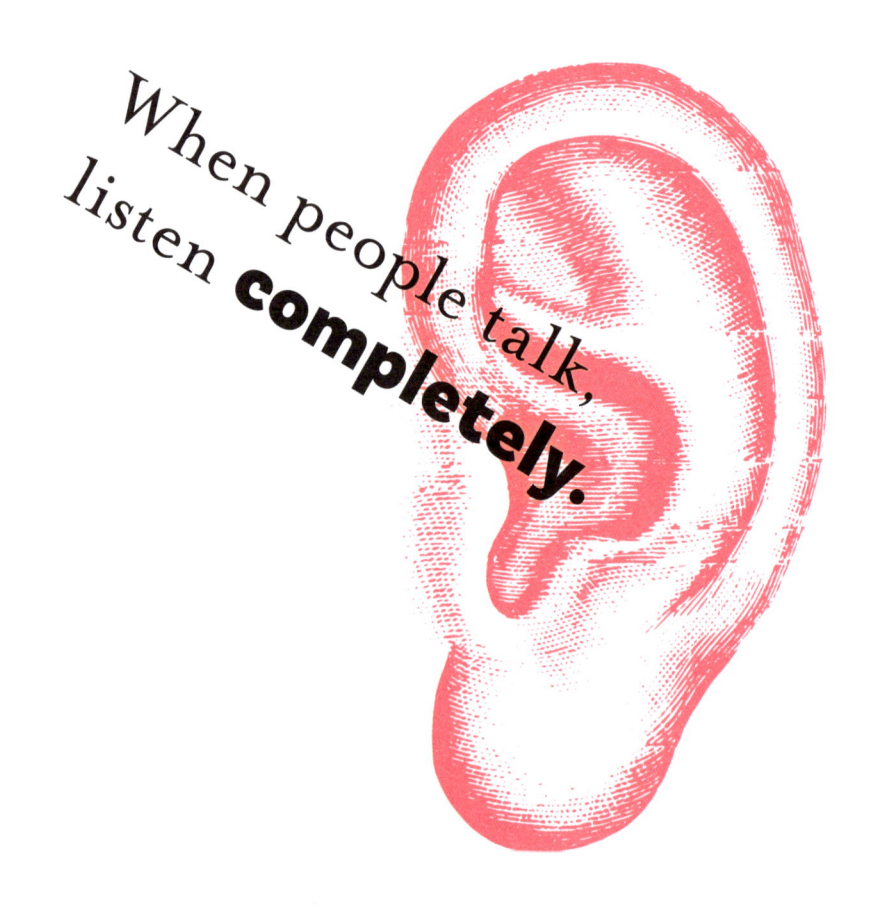

ERNEST HEMINGWAY
1899-1961

SOURCE: The article "Monologue to the Maestro: A High Seas Letter"
DATE: 1935
FIELD: Literature

American novelist and short-story writer Ernest Hemingway, probably most famous for the novels *For Whom the Bell Tolls* (1940) and *The Old Man and the Sea* (1952), won the Nobel Prize for Literature in 1954. Yet he was almost as celebrated for his adventurous life as for his literary output: He lived in Paris among the "Lost Generation" of American expats, covered the Spanish Civil War as a journalist, was present at the Normandy landings and the Liberation of Paris in the Second Word War, lived in Cuba, and was twice nearly killed in plane crashes on safari in Africa.

His advice here is from a piece he wrote for *Esquire* magazine in 1935, "Monologue to the Maestro: A High Seas Letter." He wrote, "When people talk, listen completely. Do not be thinking what you are going to say. Most people never listen." Good communications skills are often stated as a requirement for leadership positions, and listening well is a key component of communicating. Yet none of us should take listening for granted; for one thing, people with really good concentration are rarer than we might think. As we all know, it is easy to find your mind wandering during a discussion. Sometimes, as Hemingway suggests, you may find your mind running ahead and planning a response before you have really taken in what the other person is saying. You may actually miss the point of their statement. When in discussion or negotiations, give the other person your undivided attention.

Character cannot be developed in ease and quiet. Only through experience of trial and suffering can the soul be strengthened, ambition inspired, and success achieved.

44

HELEN KELLER
1880–1968

SOURCE: *Helen Keller's Journal*
DATE: 1938
FIELD: Activism

American author and activist Helen Keller was the first deaf-blind person to earn a BA degree. She was a widely inspirational figure. Deaf and blind following a serious illness at the age of 19 months, she was educated by a young teacher, Annie Sullivan, from the Perkins Institution for the Blind in Boston—as celebrated in a Pulitzer Prize-winning play and Academy Award-winning movie, both called *The Miracle Worker*. After studying at Radcliffe College in Cambridge, Massachusetts, she began to write about her blindness and other subjects for magazines, including the *Ladies' Home Journal* and *The Atlantic Monthly*, and later authored several books, among them *The Story of My Life* (1903), *The World I Live In* (1908), and *Helen Keller's Journal* (1938).

Clearly Keller had a very challenging life and wrote from personal experience in the quote opposite, from the *Journal*. Her words are deeply inspirational for us at times when we are faced with setbacks and disappointments. They remind us that through difficulty we develop our capacity to endure. Biographies of great leaders and business figures often describe failures. These people learn from what has gone wrong, and direct their attention forward, determined to do better next time. The key lies in the attitude a person adopts when faced with difficulty. As Keller says, setbacks inspire ambition and "strengthen the soul"—that is, they help us develop our deepest resources. It is through failing that we gain the strength to succeed, through losing that we find the way to win.

You just can't beat the person who never gives up.

BABE RUTH
1895–1948

SOURCE: Article in *The Rotarian*
DATE: 1940
FIELD: Sports

Arguably the most famous American athlete of all time, Babe Ruth, byname of George Herman Ruth, Jr., was a baseball star for the New York Yankees who scored 714 home runs across a career lasting from 1919 to 1935. His exploits included becoming the first man to hit three home runs in one game—in the 1926 World Series—and the following year scoring 60 home runs in one season, a record that stood until 1961.

He made the statement opposite in an article written in 1940 for *The Rotarian*, a magazine published by the civic organization Rotary International. He wrote that in baseball a player never gives up until he is actually given out, so if he is running for first base but it looks as though he will not make it, he still sprints his absolute fastest. As in baseball, so in life, he says: Do not give up because you begin to doubt you are going to make it. The same goes if you feel no one is backing you, or you face a setback. In the article Ruth makes a comparison with Henry Ford, who, he wrote, kept going in the early days, despite ridicule. Determination is a great quality in a leader. We have seen, in our discussion of other key leadership quotes, that persevering blindly in the face of bad feedback or negative developments is not helpful. The point here is not that we should persevere despite everything, but be determined and not easily put off.

The price of greatness is responsibility.

WINSTON CHURCHILL
1874–1965

SOURCE: Speech at Harvard University
DATE: September 6, 1943
FIELD: Wartime leadership

Winston Churchill is often celebrated as the greatest leader of the 20th century. He was the wartime prime minister who led Britain from looming defeat in summer 1940 to victory over Nazi Germany. He was a great writer (winner of the Nobel Prize for Literature in 1953), orator, and figurehead. He was dogged, determined, and seemingly unbreakable, a pragmatist. In his own colorful language, his policy was to "keep buggering on," meaning respond to the situation and just keep going. Never give up.

He made the statement opposite on September 6, 1943, in a speech while receiving an honorary degree at Harvard University. In the context of the Second World War he was referring to Americans and their "responsibility" to take part in defeating Nazism in the Second World War: If Americans had not become a great people, they would have been free to ignore global events, but since they have become great, they must not duck their duty—"The people of the United States cannot escape world responsibility."

The same point applies to us as leaders. If we have risen to a position of preeminence as leaders, we must take responsibility for our role, the company or organization we represent, and the people who work for and with us. The best leaders, as we know from experience as followers, are those who take the role seriously and pay attention to the needs of their subordinates. People also have responsibility to their own greatness—their abilities and ambition; they should not duck their duty to make the most of themselves.

Never tell people how to do things. Tell them what to do and they will surprise you with their ingenuity.

GENERAL GEORGE PATTON
1885–1945

SOURCE: Patton's posthumously published memoir, *War As I Knew It*
DATE: 1947
FIELD: Generalship

Bluff US general George Patton played a major role in the Second World War. He took part in the Allied invasion of North Africa in 1942, led the 7th Army's attack on Sicily the next year, and commanded the 3rd Army in France and Germany following the June 1944 Normandy invasions. He was known for swift, aggressive tank warfare and for his colorful leadership, including delivering inspiring, profanity-laden speeches to his troops. A talk he gave to the 3rd Army on June 5, 1944, the day before the Normandy invasions, has been celebrated as one of history's greatest motivational speeches.

Patton delivered the advice opposite in his memoir *War As I Knew It*, published posthumously in 1947—he died aged just 60 from injuries sustained in a car crash in December 1945. In his style of leadership, motivation was key and results were all—how things were achieved did not matter. This is obviously not true for all of us. Clearly, for some leaders, how your team-members or colleagues do the work you assign them is very important; in some roles there are prescribed methods of working and people have to stick to the rules. Yet Patton's advice is a useful warning against micromanaging. For success as a leader, we need to develop the capacity to delegate and trust people to perform. What is more, trusting people to find a way is part of an enabling style of leadership in which leaders give people confidence and draw out their capacity to succeed.

My life is my message.

MOHANDAS GANDHI
1869-1948

SOURCE: A note written to a journalist
DATE: September 7, 1947
FIELD: Nonviolent resistance

Indian lawyer and nationalist leader Mohandas Gandhi was one of the most transformative figures of the 20th century—a key player in India's gaining independence from the British Empire in 1947, whose fellow Indians granted him the honorary name Mahatma ("Great Soul"). In the face of British colonialism Gandhi developed a strategy of nonviolent resistance, *satyagraha* (keeping to the truth), that was a major influence on US civil rights leader Martin Luther King, Jr., and others struggling against racism and violence around the world. In satyagraha, he said, people facing injustice had a duty to resist, but the resistance should not be defiant and should have "no ill will or hatred behind it"; the object was "to convert, not to coerce, the wrongdoer."

Gandhi wrote the words opposite on a piece of paper when asked by a journalist in Calcutta whether he had a message. Gandhi called himself a "practical idealist." He said the simple principles by which he lived—nonviolence and truth—were as old as the hills, and the only way to spread them was to live them. He never expected his followers to do anything that he would not do himself. Leaders like this, those who live out their values, are truly inspirational. As discussed elsewhere in the book, we should model the kind of behavior we want to see in those who work with and for us. The people see that you are really committed to a shared enterprise, and this builds powerful loyalty.

> Success belongs to those who act bravely without being afraid of consequences.

JAWAHARLAL NEHRU
1889–1964

SOURCE: Reported saying
DATE: ca. 1947
FIELD: Politics

One of the key leaders of the Indian independence movement in the 1930s and 1940s, Jawaharlal Nehru was the first prime minister of independent India from 1947 to his death in 1964. He was a close associate of Mohandas Gandhi (see page 101) and was greatly influenced by him. As prime minister he stressed the importance of modern ways and a secular rather than religious approach for India.

The Gandhian policy of *satyagraha* (keeping to the truth) is built on the approach embodied in this quote: You will succeed if you do the right and necessary thing and do not worry about the results. Such an attitude makes people brave. You take the decision to act and to accept the consequences. Between 1921 and 1945 Nehru was imprisoned nine times while following Gandhi's policy of determined, peaceful resistance to the injustices of British imperial rule, serving a total of nine years' jail time.

This approach also casts a penetrating light on the problem of means and ends. In this view, "ends" grow naturally out of "means" and cannot be separated. You should never consider using the wrong means to reach the right end—you should not do a small wrong to achieve a greater right; instead you should focus on the means and not the end. Do the right thing and let the result take care of itself. This approach enables leaders to be decisive and effective, an embodiment of inspirational leadership: Choose the right path and commit yourself and your team to it, and then move on to the next decision.

One cannot accomplish anything without fanaticism.

EVA PERÓN
1919–1952

SOURCE: Reported saying
DATE: 1949
FIELD: Argentinian politics

Former actress Eva Perón was a formidable political force in Argentina in the mid-20th century, campaigning beside her husband Juan Perón as he won elections as president in 1946 and 1952 and serving in an unofficial capacity in his first government. Better known as "Evita" (the diminutive form of Eva), she made a strong connection with the poor working class of her country—the so-called *descamisados* ("shirtless ones")—and established a welfare foundation that proved a major force for change. By 1952, when she died aged just 33 of cancer, she was known as the "Spiritual Leader of the Nation." She was internationally famous and after her death her celebrity was reinforced by the 1976 rock concept album *Evita* by Andrew Lloyd Webber and Tim Rice that became a smash-hit Broadway and London show and then a movie in 1996 starring pop-star Madonna.

In some ways her quote is specific to her own situation. Evita rose from humble beginnings and became a powerful woman in a conservative, male-dominated society. She was fighting the status quo; Cristina Kirchner, the first woman elected Argentine president, in 2007, said Evita was an inspiration, an "example of passion and combativeness." As leaders there will be times when we all need the drive—what she calls fanaticism—to get things done. Fanaticism gives you the perseverance celebrated by Babe Ruth (see page 95). With fanaticism you have total belief in what you are trying to achieve, and from this stems the passionate combativeness celebrated by Cristina Kirchner.

> A good captain must be a fighter; confident but not arrogant, firm but not obstinate; able to take criticism without letting it unduly disturb him.

SIR DON BRADMAN
1908-2001

SOURCE: *Farewell to Cricket*
DATE: 1950
FIELD: Sports

Australian cricketing hero Don Bradman, arguably the greatest batsman in the history of the game, was known for his modesty, integrity, and dignity, as well as for his immense natural talent, superb concentration, and determination to win. Across his career he scored 6,996 runs for Australia in Test (international) matches, at an average of 99.94 runs per innings. He knew a thing or two about leadership: As captain of the 1948 Australian team that went through an entire tour of England without losing and won the Test series 4-0, he said he was "like a father," head of "a team of cricketers whose respect and loyalty were unquestioned, who would regard me in a fatherly sense and listen to my advice."

His advice opposite casts good leaders as sure of themselves, confident in their ability and authority, but not brittle or self-regarding. They can take criticism because their authority is not in doubt or under threat in any way. Interestingly, he said of the triumphant 1948 tour team that the fact that team members had unquestioning loyalty and saw him as a father figure created a sense of freedom and liberated them to make the most of their creativity. Like a father (or mother)—this is an intriguing model for the leader. Like parents, leaders want to make their "children" in the team or company realize their abilities and find fulfillment. The leaders want to establish a warm, supportive, respectful atmosphere, like that of the best families, one in which people feel safe to take risks.

Out of clutter find simplicity;
from discord find harmony;
in the middle of difficulty
lies opportunity.

ALBERT EINSTEIN
1879–1955

SOURCE: Reported saying
DATE: ca. 1950
FIELD: Science

German-born American physicist Albert Einstein transformed our understanding of the universe with his theory of relativity and the world-famous equation $E = mc^2$, which expresses the equivalence of mass and energy. He won the 1921 Nobel Prize in Physics, came to the United States because as a Jew he was threatened by the rise of the Nazis in Germany, and worked at the Institute for Advanced Study at Princeton. Einstein's saying was reported by theoretical physicist John Archibald Wheeler in *Cosmic Search* magazine in 1979.

Difficulty often brings opportunity. For one thing, when a situation unravels it has to be put back together. If you take a positive approach, you can often impress your leadership skills on others by the way you respond. You might even be able to improve your own position or that of the team you are leading as part of the restructuring. It's often when you are "in the middle of difficulty"—when you get stuck thinking through a problem—that inspiration strikes.

When you are stuck in this way, put your work aside. Take a walk; pledge to come back to the task the next morning. The quote contains another great piece of leadership advice: Find simplicity. This can apply, as we have seen, to limiting your commitments, so that you have time to get to know your colleagues and to take an overview of the organization and its work. It can also apply to the work itself and what you produce. Make it as simple as possible. Really focus on the core question.

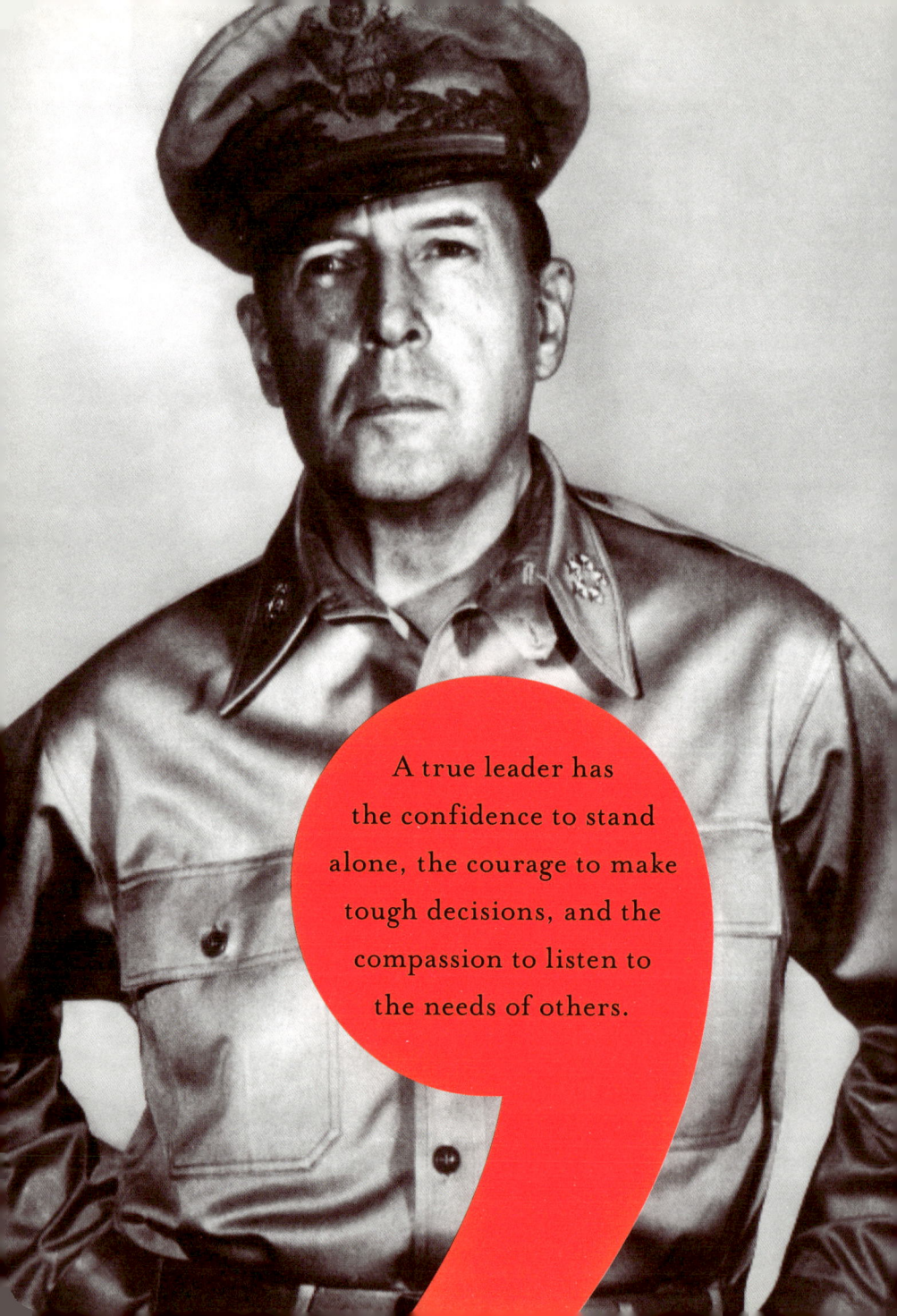

A true leader has the confidence to stand alone, the courage to make tough decisions, and the compassion to listen to the needs of others.

DOUGLAS MACARTHUR
1880-1964

SOURCE: Reported saying
DATE: ca. 1951
FIELD: Military

Douglas MacArthur was a major figure in the US Army in the Second World War. As commander of US forces in the Far East, he was in charge of the retaking of the southwest Pacific in 1942–45, then after Japan surrendered he took control of the Allied administration of the country from 1946 to 1951. He later entered the corporate world, becoming chairman of the board of office machines firm Remington Rand. He is remembered as something of a controversial figure, who was relieved of his command of United Nations forces in Korea by President Truman because—counter to official policy—he committed to conducting a full-scale war against Chinese communists. Yet he is also celebrated for the intelligence and command skills he possessed. Leadership awards in his name are given to this day in the US Army.

His advice to leaders focuses on three key qualities: confidence, courage, and compassion. The quote opposite goes on, "He does not set out to be a leader, but becomes one by the quality of his actions and the integrity of his intent." His vision is not of an individual thrusting himself forward as a leader because he loves power or its trappings, but one who demonstrates leadership by the way he treats others and by living according to his core beliefs. Leaders need confidence not to be easily swayed, courage to stand up to opposition when necessary, to make decisions and stand by them. They win the love and loyalty of colleagues and followers through their compassion, by showing they understand and care for their teams.

You must do the thing you think you cannot do.

ELEANOR ROOSEVELT
1884–1962

SOURCE: *You Learn by Living*
DATE: 1960
FIELD: Diplomacy and humanitarianism

Eleanor Roosevelt was the niece of President Theodore "Teddy" Roosevelt and wife of President Franklin D. Roosevelt (FDR). She was first lady of the US from 1933 until 1945, then, after the death of FDR in 1945, a delegate to the United Nations, where she played a major part in the drafting of the Universal Declaration of Human Rights in 1948. The quote opposite comes from her 1960 book *You Learn by Living* and is part of a statement in which she urges people to face up to their fears: "You gain strength, courage, and confidence by every experience in which you really stop to look fear in the face. You are able to say to yourself, 'I have lived through this horror. I can take the next thing that comes along.' [...] You must do the thing you think you cannot do."

As leaders, we cannot allow ourselves to be fearful of change or challenges. It is very important for our own development, and our leadership of others, that we know we can face up to major challenges and show others that we are confident and capable. Roosevelt's point goes beyond this to state that the fact that we have faced up to something we feared makes us stronger next time. We have proven to ourselves that we can overcome nerves and fear and survive whatever the challenge may bring. Think of your own experience of a teacher, manager, or other leader who faced up to a major challenge, and of how impressed you were by that.

Courage—not complacency—is our need today. Leadership—not salesmanship.

JOHN F. KENNEDY
1917–1963

SOURCE: Speech accepting Democratic Party nomination for the presidency
DATE: July 15, 1960
FIELD: American presidency

John F. Kennedy was a youthful, glamorous, charismatic, and very popular president, whose assassination in Dallas on November 22, 1963, shocked the world. He delivered the words opposite in his speech in Los Angeles on July 15, 1960, accepting the Democratic Party nomination for the presidency, a speech famous for his declaration, "We stand today on the edge of a New Frontier." The words come from a part of the speech where he is contrasting rhetoric with actions and decisiveness. At a time when it might seem easier "to be lulled by good intentions and high rhetoric," he called on people to be pioneers. He said, "I believe the times demand new invention, innovation, imagination, decision." He went on to state that "the only valid test of leadership is the ability to lead—and lead vigorously."

Kennedy was emphasizing the dynamic part of leadership. As leaders we need good rhetorical skills to be compelling public speakers and convincing in meetings. Yet we also need energy and dynamism, "the new invention, innovation, imagination" that JFK was describing. Leaders are responsible for driving change and achievement. We need to be able to convince people who think they are operating at the peak of their abilities to achieve more. We see potential improvements or opportunities that others may miss. When appropriate, we should give rein to our dynamism, to our ideas and passion, to the energy that fired us up to be on this path in the first place.

A true leader always keeps an element of surprise up his sleeve.

CHARLES DE GAULLE
1890–1970

SOURCE: Reported saying
DATE: ca. 1960
FIELD: Statecraft

Charles de Gaulle was the combative, inspirational leader of the Free French forces in exile in World War II and then president of France from 1958 to 1969. He was brave and supremely self-confident—when Allied troops liberated Paris from the Nazis in 1944, he rode in triumph down the Champs Élysées in the city and strode publicly into Notre Dame Cathedral, despite the fact that survivors of the wartime regime that had collaborated with the Germans tried more than once to shoot him.

De Gaulle's advice to leaders was, do not let other people feel they always know what you are going to do. Keep things fresh. The words opposite are part of a longer quote that reads in full, "A true leader always keeps an element of surprise up his sleeve, which others cannot grasp but which keeps his public excited and breathless." He said, "others cannot grasp" your action—they cannot pin you down or predict you. Your reputation for making unexpected interventions keeps people interested; it may make you seem creative.

This is a different angle on leadership from any we have come across in the book so far: it is both about managing your image and keeping your thinking and actions fresh. To be able to intervene in this way a leader needs distance: She needs to have time away from the day-to-day management of a situation to recharge her batteries, develop creative ideas, plan strategy, and develop long-term approaches. If you have this distance, you can keep a surprise up your sleeve in the way de Gaulle proposes.

The true revolutionary is guided by a great feeling of love. It is impossible to think of a genuine revolutionary lacking this quality.

ERNESTO (CHE) GUEVARA
1928-1967

SOURCE: Article in *Marcha* magazine
DATE: March 12, 1965
FIELD: Revolutionary activism

Activist and author Che Guevara took part alongside Fidel Castro in the Cuban Revolution of 1956–1959 and was then a guerrilla leader in South America. Shot by the Bolivian army in 1967, he became an enduring icon of revolutionary struggle: A 1960 image of him, long-haired, bearded, and wearing a beret, has adorned a thousand student walls and T-shirts from the time of his death onward. The quote opposite comes from an article he wrote in 1965—"From Algiers, for *Marcha*. The Cuban Revolution Today" was an open letter to Carlos Quijano, editor of a Uruguayan weekly publication, *Marcha*. He wrote that a revolutionary, while totally committed to the revolution, needed a "large dose of humanity": "We must strive every day so that this love of living humanity is transformed into actual deeds."

In this context, the love he writes of is an emotion with a practical expression. It is the energy that drives action. As leaders effecting change in our organizations we need to be attuned to the needs of those we lead, to the effects for them of any changes we bring about. To bring about change, or inspire a significant achievement, we need to bring people together, to create a group mentality and buy into shared goals. Revolutionaries, Che writes, must not be driven only by dogma; they need a human connection. Leaders need to engage in a warm and genuine way with those who are working with and for them, to inspire loyalty in their followers.

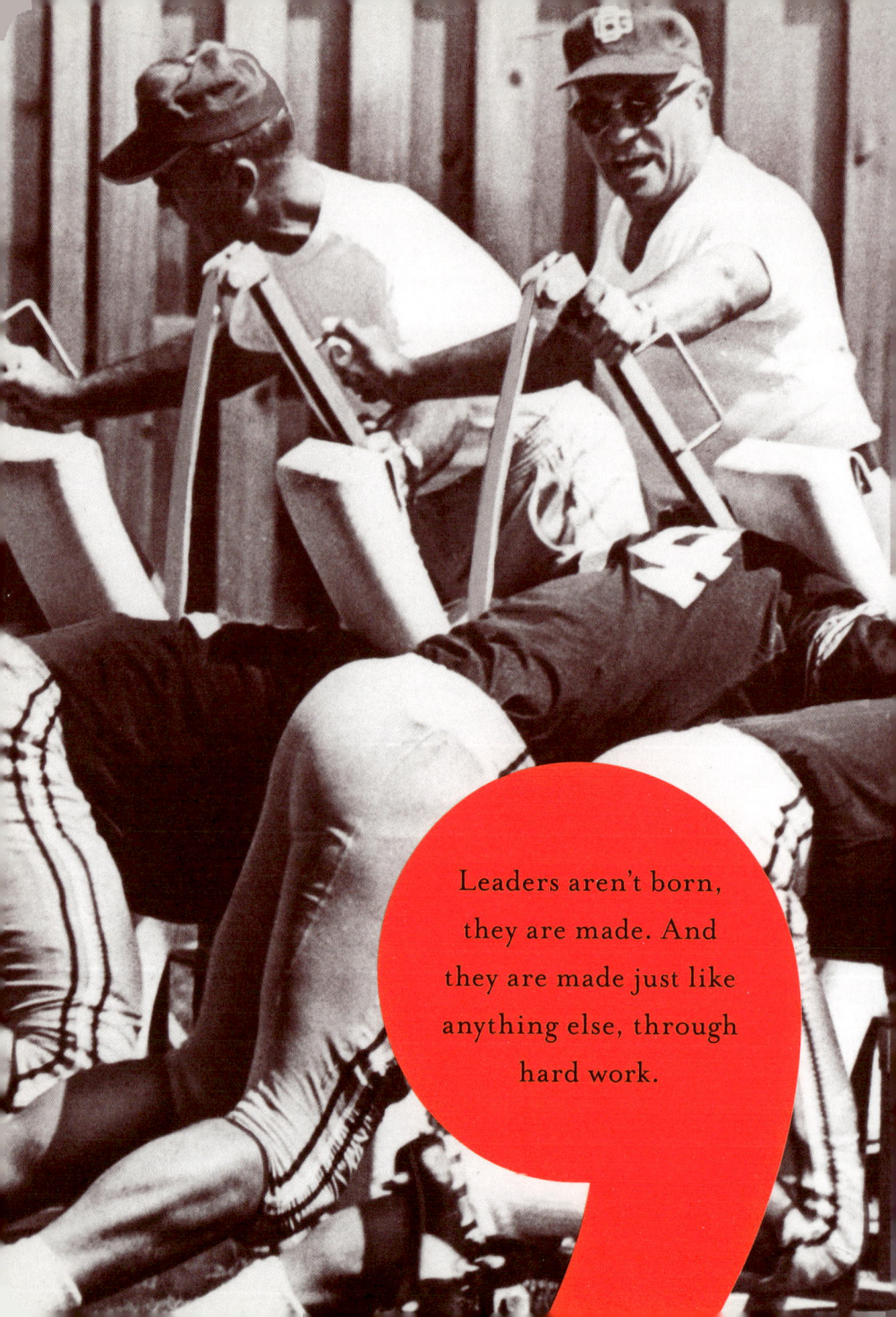

Leaders aren't born, they are made. And they are made just like anything else, through hard work.

VINCE LOMBARDI
1913–1970

SOURCE: Reported saying
DATE: ca. 1965
FIELD: Sports

Vince Lombardi is hailed as the greatest American football coach of all time, an inspirational leader who led the Green Bay Packers to five NFL championships in seven years from 1959 until 1967. Though the players changed every year, his team's success was built on discipline and unstoppable determination—what he called "a perfectly disciplined will that refuses to give in."

Lombardi was a great believer in the idea that leadership is not inborn but something you can develop. You "grow" your leadership skills through willpower and commitment—and "hard work." To be successful, he said, you have to make "a personal commitment to excellence and victory" and then each day, every week, really commit to the challenges you encounter. Winners in sport and life, he said, have to "give it everything." He told his players that the key thing was to win individual battles against the opposition: "The score on the board does not mean a thing […] You've got to win the war with the man in front of you."

Those of us who are not great athletes also need to fight and win this war—against not only our competitors but also what is holding us back, perhaps our lack of self-belief, our indolence, or our lack of judgment. His advice would be to work on the qualities we need to develop: work tirelessly and at every opportunity. This is an inspiring and hopeful perspective. We all have it in us to be excellent leaders. We only need to work at leadership to succeed in it.

You don't lead by pointing and telling people some place to go. You lead by going to that place and making a case.

KEN KESEY
1935–2001

SOURCE: Reported saying
DATE: ca. 1966
FIELD: Counterculture literature

American author Ken Kesey was a hero of the hippies in the 1960s counterculture movement in the United States. A major figure in the era's psychedelic drug culture, he traveled the US in a painted school bus with a band of drug-taking outcasts, "the Merry Pranksters." His 1962 novel *One Flew Over the Cuckoo's Nest*, set in a mental hospital, was made into an iconic 1975 movie, starring Jack Nicholson, which won five Academy Awards.

This insight is a version of "Don't tell, show"—or even, "Don't show, do." Kesey's point is that leaders who are trying to bring about change have to be part of the struggle. The best way is not to tell people, "Do it like this," but to say, "Do it like me." So Mohandas Gandhi never asked his followers to do anything that he was not willing to do himself—he was the leader in acts of civil disobedience and accepted the consequences cheerfully. Centuries earlier, Napoleon Bonaparte and Frederick the Great shared campaign hardships with their troops and won their undying loyalty.

This does not mean leaders should do everything themselves. We have spoken already about the importance of knowing how to delegate, to develop the people who work for you and show you believe in them. However, the good leader never takes refuge when the going gets tough. She is there doing the work, making the case, facing the challenge, and modeling the behavior she wants to see in her team.

> A genuine leader is not a searcher for consensus but a molder of consensus.

60

MARTIN LUTHER KING, JR.
1929–1968

SOURCE: Address at the Episcopal National Cathedral, Washington, DC
DATE: March 31, 1968
FIELD: Civil rights

Martin Luther King, Jr., Baptist minister and visionary leader of the US civil rights movement, was charismatic, strong-willed, a gifted strategist, and above all an inspirational preacher, most famous for his ringing declaration, "I have a dream that my four little children will one day live in a nation where they will not be judged by the color of their skin but by the content of their character." He was profoundly influenced by Mahatma Gandhi's *satyagraha* (keeping to the truth) in nonviolent resistance. Like Gandhi, he used the power of controlled anger at racial injustice to drive his campaign. He delivered the words opposite in an address in 1968, four years after the passing of the Civil Rights Act and his award of the Nobel Peace Prize and only days before he was assassinated on April 4 in Memphis, Tennessee.

As a leader, he was saying, you are the driving force. A good leader does not seek to be popular simply by giving people what they want. She has her own vision and the capacity to convince others that her considered way is right. It is important for your leadership to develop the rhetorical skills with which Martin Luther King was so richly blessed, so you are able to present your ideas in the most convincing way possible. Of course, it is not as simple as merely getting your own way. An important part of gaining consensus is seeking input from those you work with. That way you achieve a common purpose.

Leadership is based on inspiration, not domination; on cooperation, not intimidation.

61

WILLIAM ARTHUR WARD
1921–1994

SOURCE: Reported saying
DATE: ca. 1970
FIELD: Inspiration

Widely quoted American author William Arthur Ward wrote a column, "Pertinent Proverbs," in the *Fort Worth Star-Telegram* and also had his work published in the magazines *Reader's Digest*, *The Christian Home*, and *Science of Mind*. He worked at the Texas Wesleyan College in Fort Worth from 1955 onward and published several books, including *Thoughts of a Christian Optimist* in 1968. The quote opposite is often misattributed to William Arthur Wood.

Some leaders attempt to rule by fear: "Do this, or else." When an atmosphere like that prevails in an organization, people tend to be looking over their shoulders, anxious about making mistakes. Your team, your staff are working hard because they are afraid to fail. The focus is on individual success and failure. Yet it is better if they are working hard because they are driven to succeed, and if you have convinced them to work together with you and the rest of the team toward joint goals. This is not to say there should be no hierarchy. Some leaders are difficult to please and, depending on the qualities of the staff they are working with, this can be a great motivator. Leaders should be role models, they should have high standards to which others aspire. A certain toughness can be part of inspiring people to work together. The key, as we have seen, is to know what makes your staff and colleagues tick. As John McGraw said (see page 79), get under their skin and cater to them "with kindness or roughness as the case may demand."

You must learn to be still in the midst of activity and to be vibrantly alive in repose.

INDIRA GANDHI
1917-1984

SOURCE: Quoted in *People* magazine
DATE: 1975
FIELD: Politics

The political slogan was "India is Indira, Indira is India." Four times Indian prime minister (and the only woman to date to have been elected to that position), Indira Gandhi was a powerful leader who was highly effective under pressure and ruthless with opponents. She was not related to Mohandas Gandhi—she took her second name from her husband, the journalist Feroze Gandhi. She was the only daughter of Jawaharlal Nehru (see page 103), India's first post-Independence prime minister from 1947 to 1964 and was educated at the Shantiniketan school ("Place of Peace"), founded by the mystic and author Rabindranath Tagore (see page 83). She was a formidable figure, likened to the warlike Hindu goddess Durga.

Her words opposite deliver invaluable advice on how to perform at your best under pressure and avoid "burnout" at times when work and its challenges press in on you. To make your best decisions, as she says, you need to be able to find a place of calm amid busyness. The stillness she talks of fosters concentration and the focused attention you need to make your best decisions. Stillness also gives you space to review your strategic goals and tactics: sometimes we lose the capacity to see the overview because we are swamped with detail. Her other advice—to be alive in repose—reminds us of the need to recharge ourselves. Time away from work is absolutely necessary. It should be restful but also stimulating so that our thinking is at its best when we return to our duties primed for activity.

The task of the leader is to get his people from where they are to where they have not been.

HENRY KISSINGER
b. 1923

SOURCE: Reported saying
DATE: ca. 1975
FIELD: Politics

Henry Kissinger is celebrated for his formidable intelligence and wit, and as one of the most effective US secretaries of state of the late 20th century. He was secretary of state and national security advisor in the administration of presidents Richard Nixon and Gerald Ford from 1969 to 1977 and won the 1973 Nobel Peace Prize, with Le Duc Tho of North Vietnam, for their negotiation of the Paris Peace Accords, a settlement to end the Vietnam War. He was born in Germany but fled Nazi persecution of the Jews and immigrated to the United States in 1938. After leaving office in 1977 he became an author and consultant.

He casts the leader as someone taking others on a journey. It is true that as a leader you will sometimes have to take people into unfamiliar territory: This is when you need personal warmth and self-confidence to convince people they will succeed in a new challenge. We are back with modeling the behavior you want to see—as a leader, you need to embody self-confidence and capability. Kissinger's words might also apply to the leadership task of changing people's minds—turning around a company culture, say, or convincing colleagues of a fresh approach. We all know how damaging groupthink can be. The leader's voice challenges it. The same insight applies to driving forward creativity in the workplace. You sometimes need to go out on a limb with new ideas, risk appearing foolish or failing. As the leader you are in the vanguard, driving others forward, breaking the mold, and raising standards.

I don't run away from a challenge because I am afraid. Instead, I run toward it.

64

NADIA COMĂNECI
b. 1961

SOURCE: Reported saying
DATE: ca. 1976
FIELD: Sports

Romanian-born gymnast Nadia Comăneci was a huge star of gymnastics in the 1970s, especially at the 1976 Olympic Games in Montreal, Canada, when she became the first gymnast to be awarded a perfect score of 10/10 in an Olympic event. She won three golds, a silver, and a bronze, and overall scored no fewer than seven perfect 10s at the 1976 Games. Back home she was declared a Hero of Socialist Labor, but she defected to the United States in 1989 and became a US citizen in 2001. With her husband, former American gymnast Bart Conner, she works to promote gymnastics.

Hours and hours of practice lay behind her success. She had to develop a very strong will, as well as a strong body, to achieve such excellence. She needed to access depths of inner confidence and develop the ability to stay perfectly calm under pressure. To win she needed a determination not to be beaten—by the task or by her competitors. As her words indicate, these qualities meant that she would move toward rather than away from a challenge. This is an inspiration to us all in our leadership roles. We will benefit a great deal if we develop this attitude of "bring it on" when faced with a challenge. Then we welcome the difficulty as a way to grow and develop. Once again we will be modeling the attitude and behavior we want to see in our teams and organizations, an attitude of stepping up to the plate.

> A leader takes people where they want to go. A great leader takes people where they don't necessarily want to go, but ought to be.

ROSALYNN CARTER
b. 1927

SOURCE: Reported saying
DATE: ca. 1980
FIELD: Politics

Rosalynn Carter was first lady of the US from 1977 to 1981 as the wife of President Jimmy Carter and took an active role in his administration. She is a committed advocate for mental health and for many years she and President Carter were actively involved in Habitat for Humanity, a Christian nonprofit that built and renovated homes for those in need.

Rosalynn Carter's insight is a variation on the theme of leaders taking people on a journey: She adds a moral dimension. In her view, the best leaders are taking people where they need to go or should be going, whether or not the people want to go there. The aim must be that once there, the people will see that the new place was the right place to come to. Perhaps they could not know it was the right move to make until they had made it. Compare Mother Teresa's advice (see page 139) not to wait for others, but to make change happen; or the view of Martin Luther King, Jr. (see page 125), that as leaders we should not look for agreement but create it—mold consensus. Imagine introducing a new regulation to make working practices more equal between the sexes or between ranks in your organization—some people might resist beforehand, but then be convinced when they experience an improved working culture. As leaders we should look beyond what people apparently want and see what they need, what will benefit our team, our place of work. This is a matter of vision, a key leadership quality.

Don't follow the crowd;
let the crowd follow you.

MARGARET THATCHER
1925–2013

SOURCE: Reported saying
DATE: ca. 1985
FIELD: Britain's first female prime minister

Margaret Thatcher, Britain's first woman prime minister, was dubbed "the Iron Lady" because of her toughness and formidable, uncompromising leadership style. Prime minister for 11 years from 1979 to 1990, she was a conviction politician, who greatly valued self-reliance and argued that leaders should never try to be popular—"If you set out to be liked," she said, "you would be prepared to compromise on anything at any time, and you would achieve nothing."

Thatcher is an interesting case study in leadership because, while she was highly effective and has a number of historic achievements to her name, her unbending, "lonely at the top" style was eventually her undoing: Her refusal to back down over a very unpopular personal tax, the community charge, led to her replacement as leader of the Conservative Party and prime minister by John Major. Leaders sometimes need to be trailblazers—pioneers who make the crowd follow them.

This style of leadership can bring energy and drive to an organization, and open new possibilities of achievement. Yet leaders who pay little attention to personal dynamics—who govern through fear, say, or force of authority—often find their leadership style undermines them in the end. They may find people give up advising them, and when they are challenged, they discover they have few allies, that few people feel loyalty to them. It is interesting to note that some leaders are undermined by the very quality that takes them to power—their strength becomes a weakness. You need balance and adaptability in leadership. Do not have just the one style.

Do not wait for leaders; do it alone, person to person. Be faithful in small things because it is in them that your strength lies.

MOTHER TERESA
1910–1997

SOURCE: Reported saying
DATE: 1987
FIELDS: Charity/religion

Mother Teresa was an Albanian-born Roman Catholic nun who felt called by God to help the poor while living among them. Based in Calcutta, India, she founded and led the Missionaries of Charity, with a mission to care for "the hungry, the naked, the homeless, the crippled, the blind, the lepers." She expanded her work around the world and won the 1979 Nobel Peace Prize. In September 2016, just under 20 years after her death, she was proclaimed a saint by Pope Francis. Mother Teresa's words opposite were quoted in a 1987 book *Women of Faith and Spirit*, edited by Mary Alice Warner and Dayna Beilenson.

Her advice is: Do not put off making the change you want to see. She warns us, in effect, not to be passive, looking for someone to follow; but to be our own inspiration, to make the difference ourselves. What is more, we can make the change little by little—by being "faithful in the small things." These are truly valuable insights for leaders: Not to defer action, and to begin and proceed in small activities. We can build trust and spirit, and promote camaraderie in our organization, by being engaged with people and behaving honorably, even in the most minor engagements. In this way we will foster loyalty in the people working with and for us. Similarly, if we decide we need to make changes in ourselves, we should get to it at once: do not put off what needs to be done, but begin now and proceed "little by little."

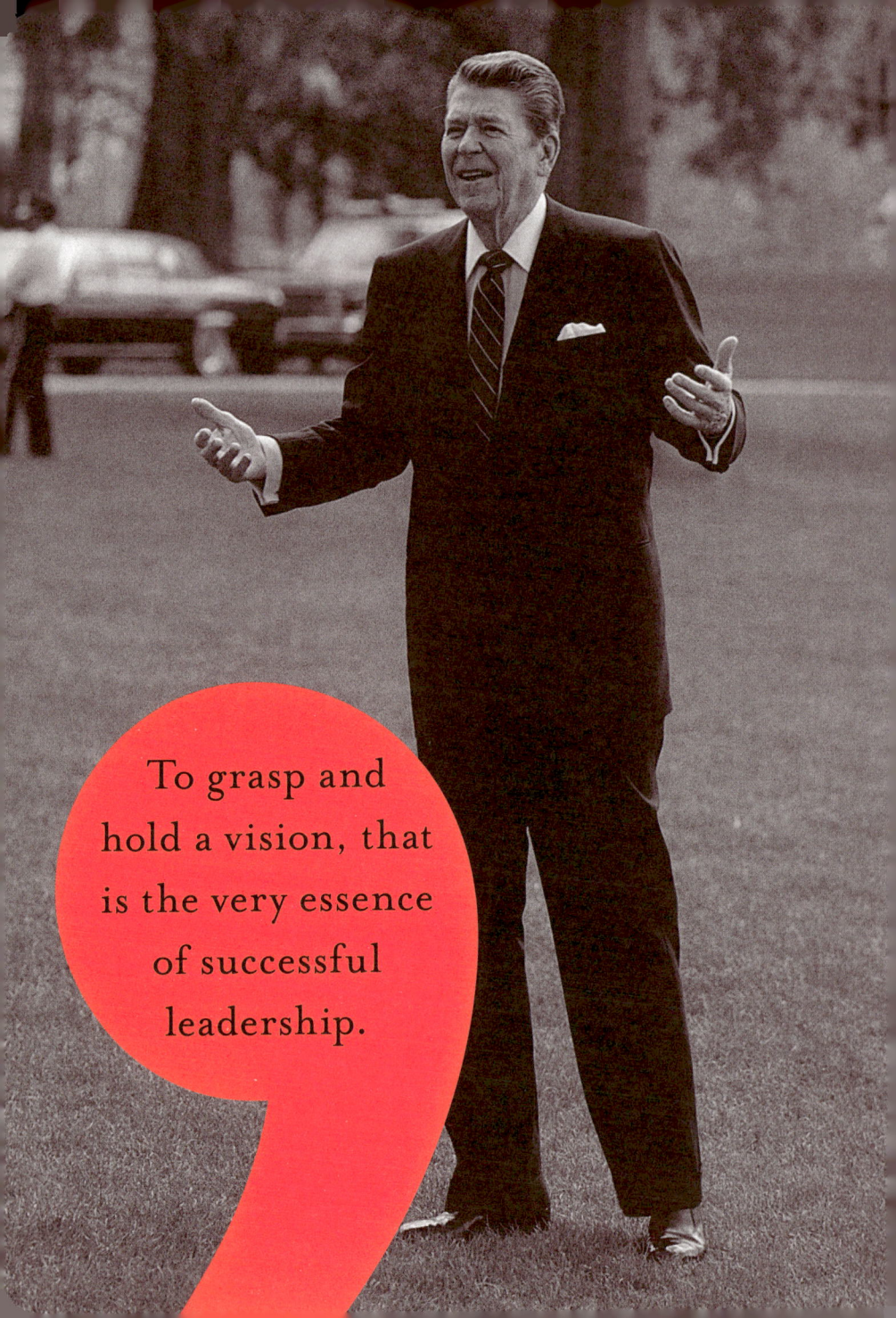

> To grasp and hold a vision, that is the very essence of successful leadership.

RONALD REAGAN
1911-2004

SOURCE: Speech in Moscow
DATE: May 31, 1988
FIELD: American presidency

Ronald Reagan had a long, successful career as an actor in Hollywood before becoming governor of California from 1967 to 1975 and then serving two terms as US president from 1981 to 1989. In Hollywood he was in scores of movies, including *Dark Victory* in 1939 with Bette Davies and Humphrey Bogart and his own favorite, *Kings Row*, in 1942. The first and so far only movie actor to become president, he had a down-to-earth appeal and was a supremely skilled speaker—winning the nickname of "the Great Communicator." He was strongly anticommunist and as president oversaw the end of the Cold War between the US and the Soviet Union.

The quote is taken from a speech he gave at a lunch hosted by artists and cultural leaders in Moscow, Soviet Union, on May 31, 1988. He said its message is applicable in all situations, "not only on the movie set where I learned it, but everywhere"—the ability to maintain and transmit a vision is a key skill for an actor in bringing the scenes in a script to life, but also for a leader in communicating meaning and inspiring people to follow. He added that he recognized the same skill in Soviet leader Mikhail Gorbachev and this enabled them to find "respect" and work together effectively. As leaders we are often the carriers of the vision for the group. In this aspect of their role, leaders ensure that work is relevant to the goal and maintain morale. They keep their organization on track.

> As we look ahead [...] leaders will be those who empower others.

69

BILL GATES
b. 1955

SOURCE: Reported saying
DATE: ca. 1990
FIELD: Business

American computer mogul Bill Gates cofounded Microsoft with his friend Paul Allen in 1975. They adapted the BASIC computer programming language used on large mainframe computers for early personal computers and subsequently licensed MS-DOS (Microsoft Disc Operating System) to the IBM office machine company. Through this, the later Windows computer operating system, and his company Corbis, Gates made a personal fortune that ran into tens of billions of dollars. He is celebrated for his flexibility and business acumen. In 2000 he and his wife founded the Bill and Melinda Gates Foundation; they are among the world's greatest philanthropists.

In an era when jobs are less secure and the old idea of a job for life with one company does not apply any more, workers have a particular need to be developing skills and confidence so they can be proactive about building a career across different organizations. Empowering your colleagues and team members is an ever more necessary part of modern leadership. It is important to ensure you share tasks and delegate effectively, that you encourage ownership of decisions and teamwork. Give feedback regularly. Your colleagues benefit by gaining skills in a supportive environment, and you benefit because they are happier in their job and likely more productive. Allowing colleagues input in creative discussions or decision-making builds an engaged team. You may also improve the quality of the creative decisions. Another important part of empowering workers, as we have seen, is ensuring you know them well: It will help you give them effective guidance.

The art of leadership is saying no, not saying yes. It is very easy to say yes.

TONY BLAIR
b. 1953

SOURCE: Interview
DATE: 1994
FIELD: Politics

Tony Blair was British prime minister for ten years between 1997 and 2007. Aged just 43 when elected prime minister in a landslide victory, he was the youngest prime minister since 1812 and was initially very popular; he won two further elections in 2001 and 2005. After standing down he served as envoy to the Middle East on behalf of the European Union, the US, Russia, and the United Nations in 2007–15, then in 2017 launched the Tony Blair Institute for Global Change as a policy platform designed to fill the middle ground in British politics.

The quote opposite comes from an interview he gave as British Labour Party leader in October 1994 before becoming prime minister. He encountered a good deal of opposition when "rebranding" the party as he moved it toward the center ground politically. His statement delivers a useful insight: Leaders have a duty to stand against what is deemed popular if necessary. They are often the ones taking a strategic view and that may require tactical decisions that have long-term benefits but are difficult to accept in the short term. Another aspect: As a leader you may need to say "no" to calls on your time in order to ensure you can step aside from the day-to-day to engage in the strategic and tactical thinking just described. Take a pencil and draw through events in your diary that do not require your presence and those that, while they may be pleasant, do not bring you any long-term benefit. Free yourself by saying "no."

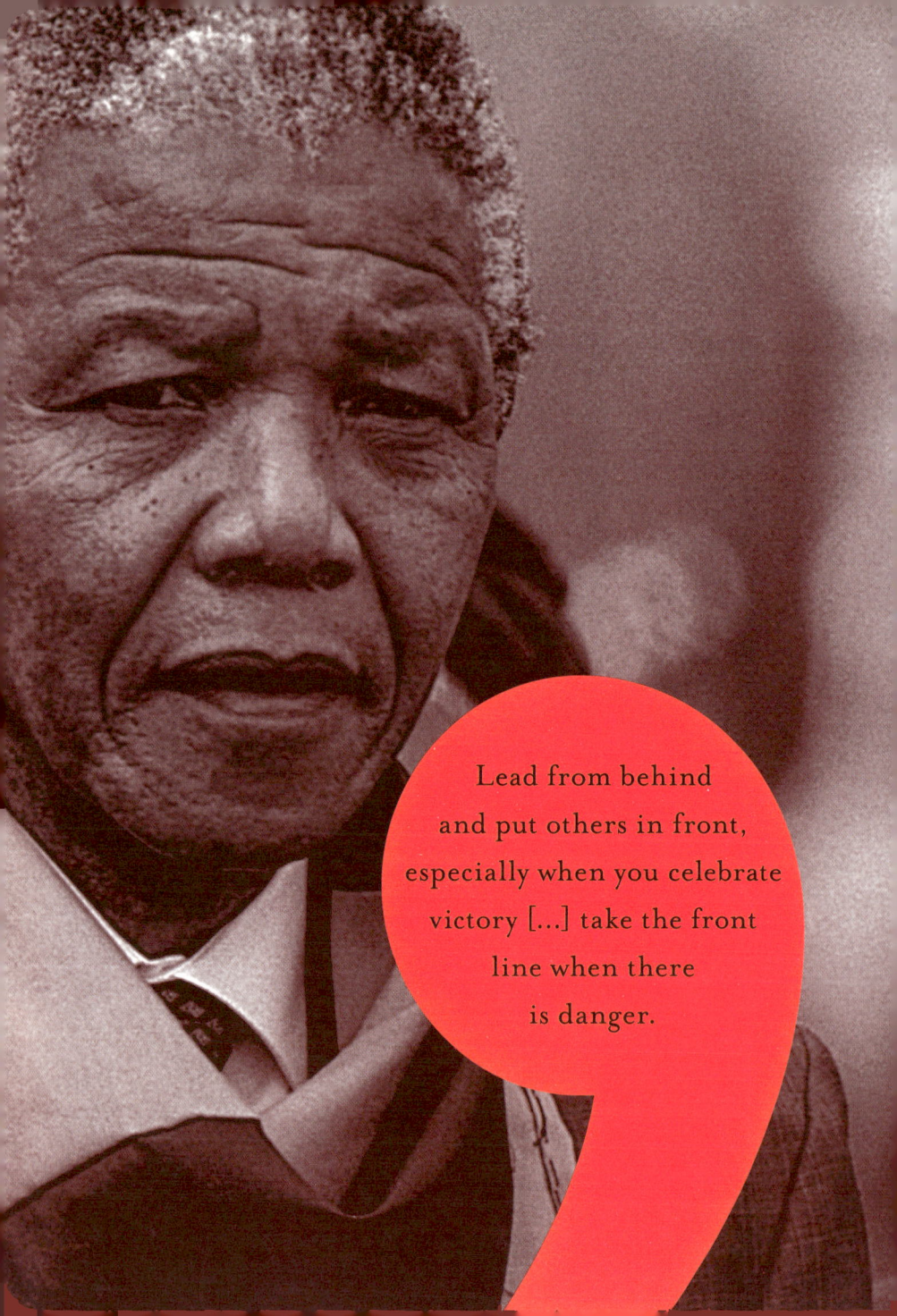

> Lead from behind and put others in front, especially when you celebrate victory [...] take the front line when there is danger.

NELSON MANDELA
1918–2013

SOURCE: Reported saying
DATE: ca. 1994
FIELD: Statecraft

Nelson Mandela was a lawyer, anti-apartheid campaigner, leader of the black nationalist African National Congress, and president of South Africa between 1994 and 1999. He inspired the world by promoting reconciliation in his country after the years of the racially divisive system of apartheid. He put behind him his own 27 years of imprisonment from 1963 to 1982 and on his inauguration as president said, "The time for the healing of the wounds has come."

The words opposite are extracted from a longer quote: "It is better to lead from behind and to put others in front, especially when you celebrate victory, when nice things occur. You take the front line when there is danger. Then people will appreciate your leadership," cited in *The New Yorker* and widely elsewhere. In part his insight is that you build loyalty when you ensure that colleagues and team members share in the credit for work well done, but you step forward when things are tough—you take the flak as far as is reasonable. It is partly also a matter of directing people with a light touch, in a way that they do not really notice. In his 1994 autobiography *Long Walk to Freedom*, Mandela likens the leader to a shepherd who "stays behind the flock, letting the most nimble go out ahead, whereupon the others follow, not realizing that all along they are being directed from behind." Compare Laozi's argument (see page 9) that a leader is best when "people barely know he exists" and when work is done they say, "We did it ourselves."

Leadership is solving problems. The day soldiers stop bringing you their problems is the day you have stopped leading them.

COLIN POWELL
b. 1937

SOURCE: *My American Journey*
DATE: 1995
FIELDS: Military/politics

American general Colin Powell served as national security adviser from 1987 to 1989, chairman of the joint chiefs of staff from 1989 to 1993, and secretary of state from 2001 to 2005. At the time of the 1990–1991 Gulf War he became associated with the "Powell Doctrine," under which all political, diplomatic, and economic means must be exhausted before the US turns to military action.

An important lesson of his insight into leadership is that you should ensure people can get to you with their problems. In a healthy workplace there are upward channels of communication. Make sure people can either reach you directly or get to you through a colleague. Another lesson is to take steps to establish a culture in which people are willing to admit when they need help. When people are frightened of revealing doubts or shortcomings because they think it will reflect badly on them, the organization is likely to suffer.

The quote opposite is from Powell's 1995 book *My American Journey*, which is respected in the business community for its numerous insights into leadership. It goes on to say that the soldiers stop coming to you because they "have either lost confidence that you can help them or concluded that you do not care. Either case is a failure of leadership." Of course, the practice of encouraging people to bring you their problems does not undermine your role as an empowering leader. The best leader will listen and respond, not tell team members what to do, but encourage them to find their own answers.

If your actions create a legacy that inspires others to dream more, learn more, do more, and become more, then, you are an excellent leader.

DOLLY PARTON
b. 1946

SOURCE: Reported saying
DATE: 1997
FIELD: Entertainment

Country music singer-songwriter Dolly Parton is a hugely successful businesswoman, actress, and philanthropist. She has written some of the world's most famous country music hits, including "Jolene" and "9 to 5," and starred in movies including *Steel Magnolias* (1989). She opened the Dollywood theme park in 1986 and established the Dollywood Foundation to promote education.

The quote opposite is often found on leadership forums and is frequently attributed to John Quincy Adams, the sixth US president from 1825 to 1829. However, the words are actually those of Dolly Parton in 1997, though similar ideas were expressed by earlier individuals. Her insight is that a person's legacy as a leader lies not only in work achievements, but also in inspirational effects on others. Think back to a teacher who inspired you at school or college: more important than the results she achieved is the way her influence has run through your life and those of others.

The leader Parton envisages is an empowering individual of the kind referred to by Bill Gates (see page 143), someone who encourages others to make the most of themselves, but particularly an inspiring individual. This aspect of your leadership role is partly about what you say and partly about how you behave. Are you positive? Do you assign blame or seek solutions when things go wrong? Do you carry on looking for ways to learn and achieve more yourself? Do you show your people how to look beyond immediate tasks to larger goals? As a leader you are a role model.

It is only by being **bold** that you get anywhere. If you are a risk-taker, then the art is to protect the downside.

RICHARD BRANSON
b. 1950

SOURCE: *Losing My Virginity*
DATE: 1998
FIELD: Business

British entrepreneur Richard Branson founded Virgin Records in 1973, was the main backer of the Virgin Atlantic airline in the 1980s, and by the 1990s had around 100 businesses in his Virgin stable. He built a vast fortune and is known as a sporting risk-taker in powerboats and hot-air balloons. The quote comes from his 1998 autobiography *Losing My Virginity*, from a section in which he discusses taking a risk on the album *Tubular Bells* by Mike Oldfield. At this time his record company was very small—it was their first album; yet he chose not to license the promotion and distribution of the record to an established record company but to keep it in-house. If the album had failed, it might have been ruinous for Virgin; but it was a vast success—eventually selling more than 13 million copies—and it really put Branson and Virgin on the map.

So he knows all about taking risks. People admire a bold leader, but may lose confidence in one who is tentative and seems to lack belief in himself or the company. This is not to promote complete recklessness. As Branson says, when taking risks, you need to "protect the downside"—you have to plan for things not working out as you hope; you need an insurance policy or a "Plan B." However, as with many of the military figures we have covered—such as Napoleon or George Patton—for businesswomen and men there are times when you need to be bold, to take the battle to your opponent.

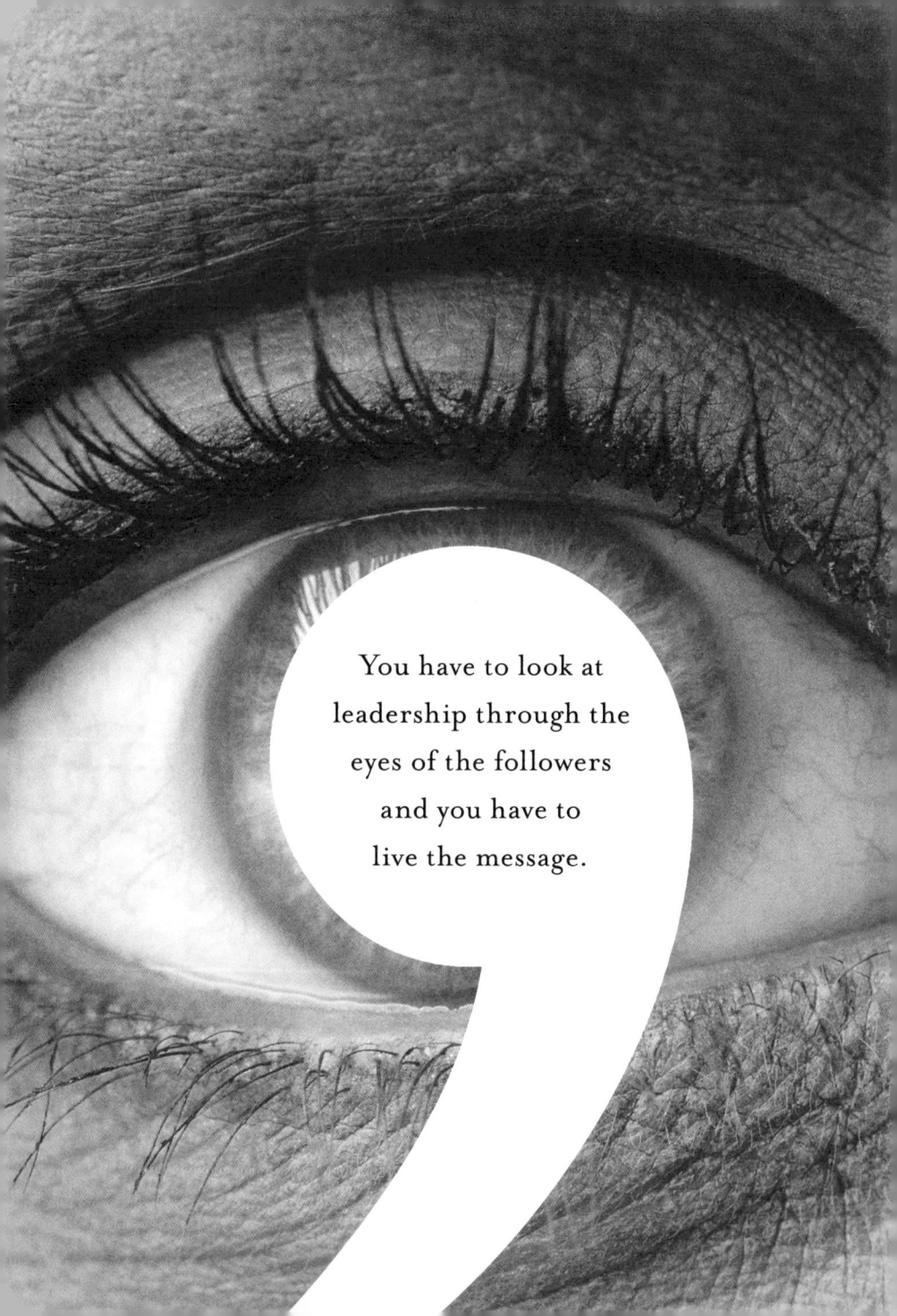

You have to look at leadership through the eyes of the followers and you have to live the message.

ANITA RODDICK
1942-2007

SOURCE: *Business as Unusual*
DATE: 2000
FIELD: Business

Anita Roddick was a British entrepreneur who founded the Body Shop cosmetics chain in 1976. She was a pioneer of ethical consumerism, promoting fair trade with the developing world and rejecting the use of ingredients tested on animals in her shops' products. By 2004 the company had 1,980 stores worldwide, and two years later she sold up to L'Oréal for £652 million (ca. $880 million). Before her death at age 64 in 2007 she gave away her £51 million (ca. $70 million) fortune to environmental and human rights groups. The quote opposite is from her autobiography, published in 2000, *Business as Unusual*.

Her insight is that our way of being is more important than our speaking. You have to "live the message"—embody the change. Think of how children are always watching their parents and teachers and very quickly spot it when the adults do something they have told children not to do. This response is just human nature, and the same applies of course to workers and colleagues— they will quickly see when you behave in a way that undermines the behavior you have called for. Seeing this, they may begin to lose respect for you. You have to practice what you preach; you have to live according to the ethos you hold. Another aspect is that when you truly live the message, your whole way of life is in line with your ideas, and you do not need to police what you say or worry about being caught out.

Knowing what must be done does away with fear.

ROSA PARKS
1913–2005

SOURCE: *Quiet Strength*
DATE: 2000
FIELD: Civil rights activism

In December 1955, African American Rosa Parks refused to give up her seat on a bus for a white man in Montgomery, Alabama, sparking the Montgomery Bus Boycott by African Americans under the leadership of local minister Martin Luther King, Jr. Parks became known as the "mother of the civil rights movement" because the year-long boycott launched the series of protests that led finally to the Civil Rights Act of 1964. Parks was active in the National Association for the Advancement of Colored People and later cofounded a career-training program for young Americans.

The words opposite—taken from the book *Quiet Strength*, a "printed record of her legacy" published in 2000—are part of a longer quote: "I have learned over the years that when one's mind is made up, this diminishes fear; knowing what must be done does away with fear." In some contexts, this is about preparation: Think ahead, be ready for the challenge. In other situations, it is about self-belief. Doubt undermines your thinking and decision-making, but being sure of your beliefs and strategy greatly enhances your effectiveness.

People—both leaders and followers—have inner reserves of strength and courage and you can more easily access these when you are certain of what you are doing and why. Imagine you feel moved to report some improper conduct in your company. Think through the issues carefully; plot your approach. Having once determined what needs to be done, and decided to do it, you can proceed without nerves or self-doubt.

All my big mistakes are when I try to second-guess or please an audience.

DAVID BOWIE
1947–2016

SOURCE: Interview in *The Word*
DATE: 2003
FIELD: Music

British singer-songwriter and actor David Bowie became one of the world's most famous rock stars. He created a series of shape-shifting personae, including Ziggy Stardust, as well as major albums from *Hunky Dory* (1971) onward. His work tended to shift between avant-garde albums, such as *Low* (1977), and more commercial records, such as *Let's Dance* (1993), and this contrast informs his comment opposite, made in an interview in 2003.

The lesson for leaders is: Be yourself. Do not get stuck trying to live out someone else's idea of what you should be doing, of what your role should be. Do it in your own way. This can apply both to the type of job you do and the way you go about it. To do something to the best of your ability you need to give it your full attention and commitment. This is why second-guessing what is needed does not deliver the best work. Your heart is not truly in it. If you find yourself falling into this trap, desperately seeking someone's approval, take a step back. Consider: What is my goal? What are my tactics for achieving it? Keep the long view in mind. Sometimes this "second-guessing" takes the form of doing things the way they have always been done, going through the motions rather than following your intuition or core beliefs. Ask yourself frequently: Why am I doing this and why am I doing it this way? Regular self-questioning is a really useful technique for leaders.

Earn your leadership every day.

MICHAEL JORDAN
b. 1963

SOURCE: Reported saying
DATE: ca. 2005
FIELD: Sports

Fans celebrate Michael Jordan as the greatest player in the history of basketball. Nicknamed "Air Jordan" because of his remarkable jumping ability, he led the US basketball team to Olympic gold medals at the 1984 Games in Los Angeles and the 1992 Games in Barcelona and took the Chicago Bulls to six National Basketball Association championships between 1991 and 1998.

Sports stars have to bring their "A game" every time they play; they know they cannot expect people to celebrate them only for what they did in the past—fans want to see them deliver today. A leader in any field should never rest on her laurels. You cannot rely on your job title, past awards, or previous project success to guarantee the respect of colleagues and team members. Leadership matters every day. You need to continually ensure you are worthy of respect. You lead by example. You meet every challenge—and convince colleagues you are a worthy leader again each time.

As we have seen, leaders do best when they have a joyful attitude to challenge. Challenges are welcome, since they provide opportunities for development and a chance to prove yourself. If you have high standards for yourself, you then have the right to apply those standards to those who work for you. Everyone in the team works to the same exacting level.

When placed in command— take charge.

NORMAN SCHWARZKOPF
1934-2012

SOURCE: Reported saying
DATE: ca. 2007
FIELD: Military

General Norman Schwarzkopf commanded the forces of the US-led coalition in the Gulf War of 1990–1991. He was known for bravery and a forthright leadership style. He could be demanding and highly critical of subordinates and stressed the benefits of training, self-discipline, and being prepared. On Schwarzkopf's death in 2012, President Obama said the general "stood tall for the country and army he loved."

His leadership insight focuses on the security a leader brings to his team when he makes it clear he is in control. Think back to your schooldays and the difference between a teacher who could control a classroom and one who could not. The one who could keep discipline created a good learning environment, right? In a way, it is liberating when a leader takes charge. A leader who is in control establishes an environment in which people can thrive and express themselves. The leader in control is like the driver of a vehicle who sets all her people free to do what they wish while she keeps the vehicle on track.

Schwarzkopf's style, as noted above, was forthright. That was his way—and he was, by all accounts, an exceptional leader. Others may choose a different way of being in charge. This is a matter of character and bearing. Schwarzkopf was also a great believer in the importance of character and said, "Leadership is a potent combination of strategy and character. But if you must be without one, be without strategy."

> We are the change that we seek.

BARACK OBAMA
b. 1961

SOURCE: Speech in Chicago
DATE: February 5, 2008
FIELD: Politics

Barack Obama served as 44th US president between 2009 and 2017, the first African American to hold the office. The quote opposite comes from a speech he gave in Chicago on February 5, 2008, Super Tuesday, during his campaign to win the Democratic Party nomination for the presidency. It is part of a longer sequence: "Change will not come if we wait for some other person or some other time. We are the ones we've been waiting for. We are the change that we seek."

Obama's words urge us to act now and not to put off hard work or difficult transformation. They encourage us to resist thought patterns such as, "I would do that, if only I could" or, "If only a great leader would arise, we could effect that change." Compare our insight from Shakespeare's *Measure for Measure* (see page 42), "Our doubts are traitors and cause us to miss the good we oft might win, by fearing to attempt." Banish doubts. If we do not try, we have no hope of success.

As leaders, we should ensure we do not give in to doubts about our own ability, and we should endeavor to support others and encourage them, drive them to achieve our shared goals. We are the ones, Obama says, who need to act. There is no reason to put things off. He says later in the same speech, "We are the hope of the future." Do not let doubts stop us, he said, "because we know what we have seen and what we believe […] Yes. We. Can."

Success is truly an inside job.

ALICE WALKER
b. 1944

SOURCE: Open letter to Barack Obama
DATE: November 5, 2008
FIELD: Literature

African-American novelist and poet Alice Walker is most famous for her novel *The Color Purple*, winner of the Pulitzer Prize in 1983 and made into a 1985 movie by Steven Spielberg. She was born in Georgia to sharecropper parents, and in the 1960s in Mississippi took part in the civil rights movement before embarking on a teaching career and becoming a writer.

The words opposite come from an open letter she wrote to Barack Obama on his becoming the first African-American president of the United States in 2008. In the letter, she argued that while he would inevitably feel enormous responsibility, he should not take upon himself sole responsibility for fixing the problems of the world. He must, she wrote, "cultivate happiness" in his life. He should "model real success" by being in a "happy, relaxed state." He could show people that "success is an inside job"—your inner qualities and attitude determine whether you succeed or fail.

These words are of profound interest to us as leaders. We have spoken elsewhere in the book about modeling the behavior we want to see in colleagues and staff; this insight takes our thinking a step further, into our way of being as people. Walker says it is essential to look after your soul, your deepest responses and beliefs, to make being the person you want to be the highest priority—"because," she writes, "finally, it is the soul that must be preserved, if one is to remain a credible leader."

A cowardly leader is the most dangerous of men.

STEPHEN KING
b. 1947

SOURCE: *Under the Dome*
DATE: 2009
FIELD: Literature

American novelist and short-story writer Stephen King has sold more than 350 million books. These have been adapted into a string of iconic movies, including *Carrie* (1976), *The Shining* (1980), *Stand by Me* (1986), and *The Shawshank Redemption* (1994). The phrase opposite is spoken by a character, newspaper editor Julia Shumway, to former army captain Dale Barbara in King's 2009 novel *Under the Dome*.

If you are in authority you have to be willing to take responsibility, not only to "face the music" when things are difficult but also to make difficult decisions for the good of the organization. Doing this ensures you have the respect of your staff and colleagues. We probably all know from experience that when leaders fail to provide leadership, when they lack authority and their people lose respect for them, the culture of an organization suffers badly. You have been overpromoted or wrongly appointed if you hide from the day-to-day demands of being a leader. You may need to act decisively to stamp out behavior that is bringing the organization into disrepute.

Of course, it is not just about being decisive—it is about acting well, making good choices. A cowardly leader is liable to take wrong decisions in order to make his own life easier. A brave leader will take the tough decisions that are needed, when they benefit the organization more than the leader herself. Being a leader is an honor and we have to make sure we are worthy of it, every day.

> Innovation distinguishes between a leader and a follower.

STEVE JOBS
1955–2011

SOURCE: *The Innovation Secrets of Steve Jobs*, Carmino Gallo
DATE: 2010
FIELD: Business

Computer pioneer Steve Jobs helped develop the iconic iPod, iPhone, and iPad, as well as the MacBook Air and other beautifully designed products that have made Apple one of the world's most admired brands. With his friend Steve Wozniak he founded Apple Computer in 1976 and they made and sold the first computer to work straight out of the box, the Apple II. He was ousted from Apple in 1985 but returned in 1996 to transform the then ailing company into a world-beater.

The quote opposite dates to 2010, the year the iPad was launched, and comes from Carmine Gallo's book *The Innovation Secrets of Steve Jobs*. Jobs' words suggest that it is the ability to come up with new and vital ideas that sets a leader apart from others. It is true that an important part of a leader's role is to be the person who does not sit back and let things drift but instead probes and pushes to see how procedures and products and relationships can be improved. In the computing and entertainment industries that Jobs knew, originality was key; for some of us it may be less important—we may need to balance originality with a commitment to reliability, we may need to be steadfast team players more than original pioneers. Innovation may be a matter of being one step ahead of what clients or the public want. Jobs and Apple never lagged behind public taste; he was a brilliant marketer. If anything, Jobs and Apple formed public taste as they went.

It takes 20 years to build a reputation and five minutes to ruin it. If you think about that, you'll do things differently.

WARREN BUFFETT
b. 1930

SOURCE: Reported saying
DATE: ca. 2010
FIELD: Business

Investor and philanthropist Warren Buffett is reckoned to be one of the richest people in the world, with a net worth of $89.5 billion as of March 2018. He is CEO of Berkshire Hathaway holding company, based in Omaha, Nebraska, and is popularly celebrated as "the oracle of Omaha." He is known for living frugally, in the same house in Omaha he bought in 1958, and has pledged to give away more than 99 percent of his vast fortune.

His quote opposite delivers a key lesson for leaders: Take the long view. Do not get swept up in the excitement of the moment. Do not be impulsive. It might also make you think: I should take advice. As we have seen elsewhere, leaders benefit from having carefully selected, able colleagues around them who are not afraid to speak their mind. Before you make a big decision, make sure you have seen more than one perspective on it. Take a moment; consider strategy, tactics. Otherwise, as Buffett says, one misstep, one hasty action can sweep away years of hard work. Of course you should not allow a cautionary insight like this to undermine your decisiveness. Nobody wants a flip-flopping, fearful leader. Try to develop your capacity to face up calmly to making decisions, weigh up pros and cons, take advice from more than one source—and then decide.

Another valuable Buffett insight is: do not get stuck in your ways. He says, "Chains of habit are too light to be felt until they are too heavy to be broken." Maintain variety, keep your curiosity. Stay nimble.

What the world is saying to us human beings is, "Don't stick to the old ways; learn to think anew."

DANIEL BARENBOIM
b. 1942

SOURCE: Interview in *The Guardian* newspaper
DATE: April 2011
FIELD: Music

Since 2009 the supremely gifted Argentine-Israeli pianist and conductor Daniel Barenboim, who has served as director of many globally renowned symphony orchestras and opera houses, has brought together young Arab and Israeli musicians in his West-Eastern Divan Orchestra. Barenboim has natural authority, on the strength of his extraordinary musical talent. He says that when he cofounded the orchestra—with Edward Said, the Palestinian literary scholar—it was as "a project against ignorance." It is essential, he argues, for people on opposite sides of the Arab–Israeli conflict to get to know one another by playing music together.

The words opposite are from a 2011 newspaper interview. He was referring in part to the way the world appeared to be changing rapidly with the then recent Arab Spring of protests in the Middle East and North Africa. He went on, "And that's what musicians do every day. You do not go out and play Beethoven's Opus 111 without having rethought about it every time you play." (Beethoven's Opus 111 is his last piano sonata, No. 32.) As leaders, "thinking anew"—coming up with fresh ideas and approaches—is an important part of our role.

A key part of this innovation is learning to trust your "inner voice," your intuition. Leaders who listen in this way, who trust their intuition, can get the edge over competitors because they are difficult to predict. They are not trapped by received wisdom, but find their own path, and they are usually full of energy, because they are harnessing inner drive.

> If you want to improve the organization, you have to improve yourself, and the organization gets pulled up with you.

INDRA NOOYI
b. 1955

SOURCE: Reported saying
DATES: ca. 2011
FIELD: Business

Born in Chennai, India, Nooyi earned an MBA and began her career in India before studying at Yale and working in the US. She worked up through the ranks at PepsiCo after joining as senior vice-president of strategic planning in 1994. She became the first female CEO of PepsiCo in 2006.

She is a great believer in communication with the workforce and writes a weekly blog. The words opposite are part of a long quote that starts with the words, "The distance between number one and number two is always a constant," meaning that the distance between me and you remains the same—so if I raise myself, you will be pulled up: If I raise my game, yours will be improved, too. She goes on, "I cannot just expect the organization to improve if I do not improve myself and lift the organization because that distance is a constant."

Her insight is inspirational. In what ways could you as a leader set yourself self-improvement targets? How might they inspire the people who work with and for you? It is easy to understand in terms of setting standards—if you stick to the demanding standards you have set, you can demand high standards from your staff and colleagues and from the organization as a whole. You could consider making personal improvements in terms of time management and timekeeping—perhaps in work–life balance—or, by working alongside staff, sharing the burden at a difficult time. Another Nooyi quote is, "I wouldn't ask anyone to do anything I wouldn't do myself."

Leadership is about making others better as a result of your presence and making sure that impact lasts in your absence.

SHERYL SANDBERG
b. 1969

SOURCE: Speech at Harvard Business School
DATE: April 2013
FIELD: Business

Sheryl Sandberg is the CEO of Facebook. In 2013 she published *Lean In: Women, Work, and the Will to Lead* and founded the associated nonprofit LeanIn.org to offer women "ongoing inspiration and support to help them achieve their goals." She is also known for her 2017 book *Option B*, written with psychologist Adam Grant in the wake of the sudden death of her husband Dave Goldberg, and an associated website optionb.org intended to help people "build resilience and find meaning in the face of adversity." The quote is from a speech at Harvard Business School in April 2013 to celebrate the 50th anniversary of the admission of women. Sandberg herself earned an MBA at Harvard in 1995.

Clearly we cannot—and would not want to be—everywhere in our organization. We have spoken several times in this book of the desirability and benefits of effective delegation. We want to make an impact "that lasts in our absence": Our people should be feeling the effect of our leadership when we are not there. An inspiring leader is still inspiring his associates to work hard and effectively when he is away at a meeting, on a business trip, or on vacation. In fact—and you will no doubt have examples of this in your own life—a truly inspiring leader stays with you, and you still think of him and feel his effect on your working life when you have moved on to another organization or he has retired.

One child, one teacher,
one book, one pen
can change the world.

MALALA YOUSAFZAI
b. 1997

SOURCE: Speech to the United Nations
DATE: July 12, 2013
FIELD: Education

Pakistani education activist Malala Yousafzai is the youngest person to have received a Nobel Prize. She was awarded the Nobel Peace Prize at age 17 in 2014, with Indian children's rights activist Kailash Satyarthi. Malala survived an assassination attempt at age 15 in October 2012 by the Taliban, the ultraconservative political-religious grouping who had invaded her native Swat Valley in northern Pakistan and shut down girls' schools as part of a hardline interpretation of Islamic law. After the attack she was flown to Birmingham, UK, and became a well-known international figure and campaigner, addressing the United Nations in 2013 and coauthoring a book, *I am Malala*. In 2015 she established a school in Lebanon for girls who had escaped the Syrian Civil War.

The words opposite are from the speech she gave to the United Nations on July 12, 2013, when she was urging a united effort against the forces that keep millions of children out of school—"illiteracy, poverty, and terrorism." For all of us Malala's life, courage, and words are an inspiration. She continues in her speech, "Education is the only answer. Education first." As we have seen elsewhere in this book, we develop many key elements of leadership on the job, through interaction with colleagues and the work we do on ourselves when faced with challenges and setbacks. Additionally, there is a place for training and studying. We should ensure we set aside time—both in our own schedules and in those of the staff we supervise—for self-development.

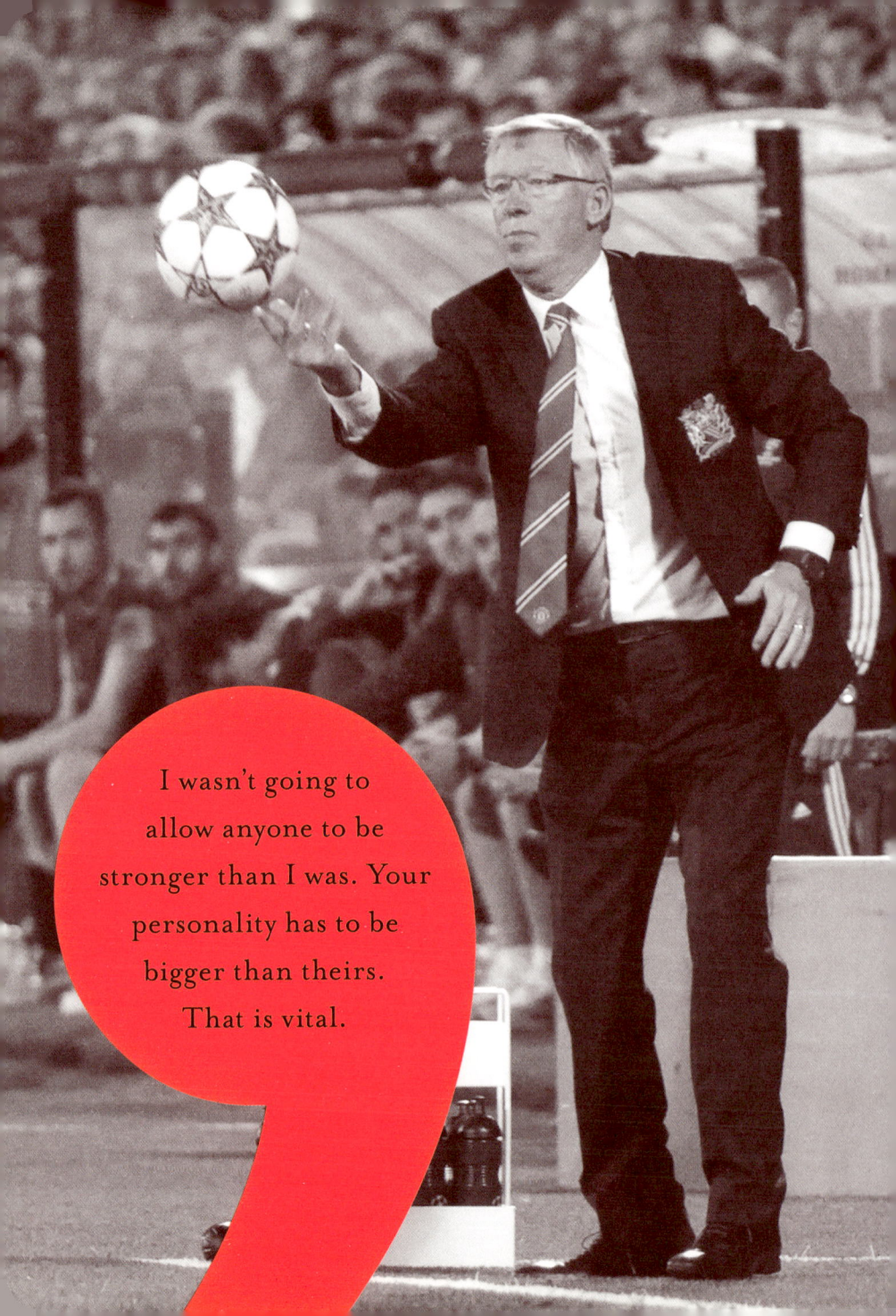

> I wasn't going to allow anyone to be stronger than I was. Your personality has to be bigger than theirs. That is vital.

ALEX FERGUSON
b. 1941

SOURCE: Interview in *Harvard Business Review*
DATE: October 2013
FIELD: Sports

The most successful manager in British soccer, Alex Ferguson won 49 trophies as manager of St. Mirren, Aberdeen, and Manchester United from 1976 to his retirement in 2013. He also managed his home country, Scotland, at the 1986 World Cup, in Mexico. He imposed his qualities—toughness, self-discipline, and drive—on the teams he built.

Ferguson was the type of manager who led through force of personality—and strict discipline. Those of us who take this approach to leadership have to make sure we are, and remain, top dog. If someone challenges you, you have to come out on top. We have seen elsewhere in this book that there are many other approaches to leadership, and many expert voices urging a different and more nuanced approach. Yet there is no doubt that this approach can work—and did work for Ferguson. He was known for taking no prisoners in disputes. He also had the highest of standards—in May 1983 he condemned as "unacceptable" the performance of his Aberdeen team, even though they had just beaten Glasgow Rangers in the Scottish Cup Final. He also recruited very cannily—signing players such as Peter Schmeichel, Eric Cantona, and Cristiano Ronaldo who were critical to his success at Manchester United. His triumphs have made him a role model for many leaders in business and sport. He has said that he maintained "hunger" through his career and presented this as an example to his players—to convince them to work hard.

The best leaders never stop learning.

DONALD T. PHILLIPS
b. 1952

SOURCE: *Lincoln on Leadership*
DATE: 2013
FIELD: Leadership studies

American author Donald T. Phillips is an expert on leadership. He has written books about the leadership of President Bill Clinton, the Founding Fathers, Vince Lombardi, and Martin Luther King, Jr., among others. The words opposite are from his 2013 book *Lincoln on Leadership: Executive Strategies for Tough Times*.

Abraham Lincoln, often celebrated as the greatest leader of them all, was known for his commitment to learning and encouraging others to learn. The best leaders engage with their colleagues and staff and are happy to share what they know with them. They are also open to learning from their subordinates. This helps stimulate innovation—the "learning culture" in an organization encourages people to try new ways of doing things. Staff will feel empowered if they see that you are taking their input seriously. Being willing to learn from your colleagues and staff is a way of showing them you respect them as people. It gives them room to grow. Compare the great Bengali poet, educator, and philosopher Rabindranath Tagore's insight: "A teacher can never truly teach unless he is still learning himself." As with teaching, with leadership, and with your work generally—to do it well you have to be alive to what you are doing, engaged with it, never just going through the motions. You should never sit on your laurels. Do not forget, too, that learning is an exciting and empowering experience. Set yourself a challenging goal. You will feel great when you achieve it.

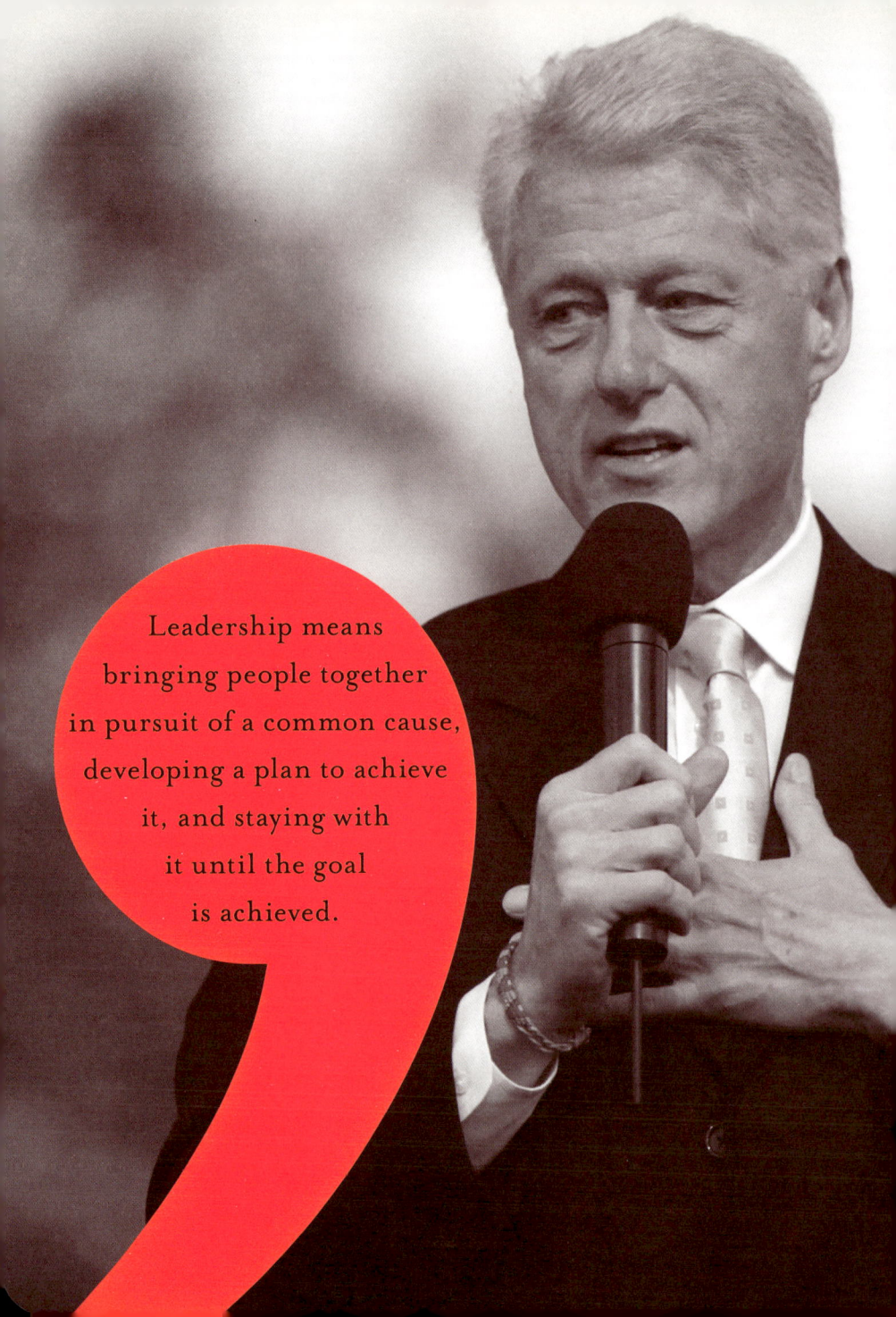

> Leadership means bringing people together in pursuit of a common cause, developing a plan to achieve it, and staying with it until the goal is achieved.

BILL CLINTON
b. 1946

SOURCE: Interview in *Fortune* magazine
DATE: April 2014
FIELD: Politics

Bill Clinton was 42nd president of the US between 1993 and 2001 and left office with the highest approval rating of any president since the Second World War after presiding over the longest spell of peacetime economic expansion in the country's history. Since leaving the White House he has carried out humanitarian work with the Clinton Foundation and served as the United Nations special envoy to Haiti after the 2010 earthquake there.

There are three crucial elements in his definition of leadership. First, we need as leaders to convince staff and colleagues that we all have a common cause. Second, we need to ensure that we come up with a defined and achievable plan. Finally, we need to "stay with it" until we have achieved what we set out to do. The first two steps in particular will work best if we adopt an inclusive style of leadership: People will buy into the organization's work if they feel they have input and their ideas are valued. In any case the inclusive leader understands that he and the organization will benefit from cooperative discussion: as Clinton says later in the interview, "Even those who lead the way do not have all the answers." "Staying with it" calls for steadfastness and courage to deal with setbacks and overcome difficulties. You may need to be brave enough to admit you were wrong and alter the plan. Then leadership calls for self-confidence, calm, and powers of persuasion to keep spirits high and ensure the team stays on track.

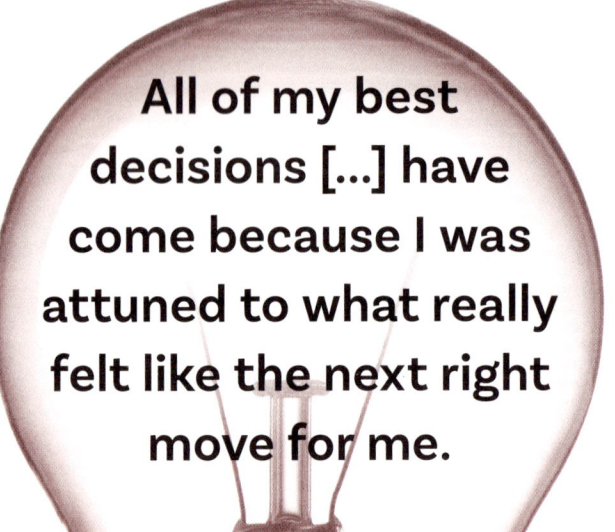

All of my best decisions [...] have come because I was attuned to what really felt like the next right move for me.

92

OPRAH WINFREY
b. 1954

SOURCE: Speech to Stanford School of Business
DATE: April 2014
FIELD: Business and entertainment

TV personality, actress, author, businesswoman, and philanthropist Oprah Winfrey is one of the most influential women in the United States. On the back of her nationally syndicated *Oprah Winfrey Show*, the highest-rated US TV talk program, she established a major media empire. She is also a successful actress, in movies from *The Color Purple* in 1985 to *A Wrinkle in Time* in 2018, and a philanthropist who opened a $40 million school for girls in South Africa.

Her comments address the role of intuition in decision-making and leadership. The words come from a speech she gave to the Stanford School of Business in April 2014: Looking back over her hugely successful career, she said, "The truth is I have from the very beginning listened to my instincts." This approach may make some of us nervous. How do you judge whether your instinct is telling you what some part of you wants to hear, or what you need to hear? Are instinctive decisions likely to be self-serving rather than really in your best interests, or those of your organization? The key element is to train yourself to be attuned to your own decision-making. We would all accept, I think, that sometimes a choice "just feels wrong." Consider your choices rationally, but also give weight to your intuitive response. Try to identify and set aside selfish elements of your response. Give yourself time when making decisions. It comes with experience. You will get to know what a good decision feels like.

We think, mistakenly, that success is the result of the amount of time we put in at work, instead of the quality of time we put in.

ARIANNA HUFFINGTON
b. 1950

SOURCE: *Thrive*
DATE: 2014
FIELD: Business

Greek-American journalist and businesswoman Arianna Huffington cofounded online magazine the *Huffington Post*, now known as Huffpost, in 2005 and continued as its editor in chief after it was bought by AOL in 2011. She stood down in 2016 to develop Thrive Global, a health and well-being startup. The advice opposite is from her 2014 book *Thrive: The Third Metric to Redefining Success and Creating a Life of Well-Being, Wisdom, and Wonder*.

Perhaps it starts at school. People get the idea that being seen to be working is the important thing. Putting long hours in pleases teacher and wins you points, but as leaders we have the opportunity to do away with the cult of "presenteeism"—in which people in an organization compete to be present at their desks longer than their colleagues. Because as the people responsible for results we know that it is the quality of work, not the number of hours, that matters. Leaders need to be fresh to work well. Our staff and colleagues will not only work better but be happier in their work and less likely to quit the organization if we create a culture that values time spent away from work—a culture that ensures people have a positive work–life balance. We need to be aware of the needs of our colleagues and staff and willing to help them with their difficulties. This approach will encourage loyalty and commitment to us and the organization. As Arianna Huffington also writes in *Thrive*, "Treat people like family and they will be loyal and give their all."

> Leadership is something you're always honing and learning and reflecting to see ways you could have been better at it.

RACHEL SKLAR
b. 1972

SOURCE: Article in *Fast Company*
DATE: June 2014
FIELD: Business

Canadian lawyer, journalist, and media figure Rachel Sklar, based in New York, is the founder of new media outlets change:the:ratio, to promote women's careers in new media and the tech industries, and TheLi.st, "a network and visibility platform for professional women from all industries." She worked for many years as a journalist, writing for the *Financial Times*, the *New York Times*, and the *Huffington Post*. The quote opposite comes from an interview she gave to American business magazine and website *Fast Company*, as part of a feature, "10 Women in Leadership Share Their Secrets to Success."

In the interview she argues against the "myth" that leaders are born not made. Far from being inborn, leadership "can be learned and should be learned." She urges a positive approach: We look at our missteps and failures to see how we can do better next time. The likelihood is that most of us excel in some aspects of leadership but leave room for improvement in others. The challenge is to ensure that we shine light on our weak areas as well as on the stronger parts of our performance. She writes, "My experience is that if you are not paying attention to the things you are doing wrong, then you are not evolving and learning." We should interrogate our performance and ensure we are open to feedback, with a focus on positive angles for improvement. We should aim to encourage a culture not of blame but growth in all forms of feedback.

Don't be afraid
to be you and
own it.

DANAE RINGELMANN
b. 1978

SOURCE: Article in *Fast Company*
DATE: June 2014
FIELD: Business

Danae Ringelmann is the cofounder and chief development officer of crowdfunding platform Indiegogo. She stresses the importance of a positive mindset: Remarkably, she and cofounders Eric Schell and Slava Rubin were rejected 90 times when trying to raise money in founding Indiegogo in 2008. She says that the key to success is in turning knockbacks into challenges.

The insight opposite focuses on the importance of authenticity. Ringelmann says that people follow you as a leader because you speak from the heart—"a true leader is someone who is wholeheartedly willing to be their authentic self." When you "own it" you commit fully to the project and this helps you be steadfast and positive. Making this commitment can be a great force for self-empowerment: You put aside self-depreciation and doubt and embody a kind of calm determination that makes you a persuasive leader and convincing negotiator. Leadership—and success—can be a matter of attitude: As Ringelmann says, you can either view knockbacks as disasters or see them as challenges. You can see difficulties and rejections as opportunities to practice a good response, to practice overcoming them. Another useful insight from Ringelmann's interview is to ask yourself why you are doing what you are doing and to expect rejections. If you have a strong, good reason for your activity this will fire you to keep going during the difficult times.

> Most people don't realize that leadership is fundamentally about service, about a dying to self and loving others into their true potential.

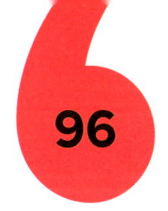

BINTA NIAMBI BROWN
b. 1974

SOURCE: Article in *Fast Company*
DATE: June 2014
FIELD: Business

Former lawyer and Harvard Kennedy School of Government fellow Binta Niambi Brown is founder and CEO of Fermata Entertainment, an artist management, development, and production company, and set up Big Mouth Records.

One key strand of leadership quotes throughout this book has emphasized the importance of nurturing employees and colleagues. You can tell a successful leader by her effect on those she works with—the measure of her success is how well she enables colleagues and others to fulfill their potential. The best leaders are not in it only for prestige or financial rewards, but because they believe in their work and in their leadership role as a means of helping others. They get their ego out of the way—as Brown says, they "die to self." They also embody the transformation they are working toward—"Be the change," as Obama said (see page 165); "Live the message," in Anita Roddick's words (see page 155).

In a separate interview with *Forbes* in 2016, Brown talked interestingly about moving from law (her first career) to the entertainment industry, where she is committed to developing work that enables personal expression and connection with communities. She described how she was excelling as a lawyer but using only "a very small portion of my spirit"; she committed to find work that she felt passionately about. She got the impetus to change and then there was no holding back—she said, "You don't have time to be afraid. It is go time."

If you're going to be a leader, you're not going to please everybody. You've got to hold people accountable.

KOBE BRYANT
b. 1978

SOURCE: *Kobe: The Interview* on NBA TV
DATE: 2015
FIELD: Sport

Playing for the Los Angeles Lakers for his entire 20-year career (1996–2016), basketball star Kobe Bryant led the NBA in scoring in seasons 2005–6 and 2006–7 and is third in the league's all-time regular season scoring chart. He won two Olympic gold medals with the US men's team at the 2008 Games in Beijing and the 2012 Games in London. Post-retirement he won an Oscar in 2017, with Glen Keane, for Best Animated Short for his movie *Dear Basketball*. He made the comment opposite during an interview on NBA TV in 2015.

Sometimes as a leader you have to drive others hard to achieve excellence. You may have to really push them. At the same time you are applying identical standards to yourself. It is a matter of building a team ethic that really works, where people accept your authority and see that you are working just as hard as they are to hit the heights. Your team understands that the pain is shared—as are the goals, and the rewards, too. You may have to forget about trying to be popular—as Kobe said, "You are not going to please everybody." Another key aspect of this is your judgment of the individuals working for you, and knowing your staff and colleagues really well. Some people respond best to being driven and directed, others to a more gentle, encouraging approach; with some, you have to be on them all the time, while others flourish if you leave them alone.

ALICIA GARZA
b. 1981

SOURCE: Quoted saying
DATE: 2015
FIELD: Politics

African-American activist and writer Alicia Garza was cofounder in 2013—with Patrisse Cullors and Opal Tometi—of Black Lives Matter, an international grouping that campaigns against systematic racism and violence against black people. Launched following the 2013 shooting of African-American teenager Trayvon Martin in Florida, the developing movement was associated with widely publicized street protests following the deaths in 2014 of African Americans Michael Brown in Ferguson, Missouri, and Eric Garner in New York City. She made the comment opposite in a 2015 interview with the Marguerite Casey Foundation, when discussing the structure of Black Lives Matter. While Garza, Cullors, and Tometi are identified as founders, the movement does not have a powerful central figure in a conventional leadership role. Some people have called it "leaderless," but Garza calls it "leader-full," commenting that "everyday people […] can be empowered to provide vision, guidance, and other forms of leadership."

As leaders we should be alert to ways in which we can help people find within themselves the skill and the confidence to lead. We have discussed elsewhere in the book the importance of encouraging input from a wide range of people, and of empowering people to develop and engage. Our organizations will benefit if we ensure that upward mobility is possible and encouraged, that people at all levels feel they are valued, can contribute, and can rise to senior positions. At a time of many challenges in the worlds of business and education—and more widely—new leadership approaches and attitudes are needed. As Garza said in 2017, "We need new leaders."

Leaders must be close enough to relate to others but far enough ahead to motivate them.

JOHN C. MAXWELL
b. 1947

SOURCE: Facebook post
DATE: January 20, 2016
FIELD: Leadership education

John C. Maxwell is a Christian pastor, public speaker, and prolific writer on leadership. He delivers talks on leadership to members of the military, business groups, government, and sports organizations and has written books that have sold in the millions, including *Developing the Leader Within You*.

His insight here is that leaders need to be both giving and demanding. Leaders who are distant from those who work with and for them may struggle to generate loyalty. What happens then when work becomes difficult, when there are challenges and setbacks? You need your people to go the extra mile, but they may be going through the motions, they may opt out. Or they may even actively work against you—seeing you vulnerable they make their move. Think of Margaret Thatcher and the way her leadership quality, initially a strength, became a weakness when she needed loyalty and support (see page 137). Yet if leaders engage with team members, if they are able to connect with their staff and colleagues, then a positive atmosphere will make good outcomes more likely. On the other hand, you sometimes need some distance—you need to be "far enough ahead to motivate them." If you are demanding and hard to please, it can motivate people to work hard.

You also have to show that you yourself have progressed along the path—of professional development and success—that you expect your staff to follow. This is leading by example: inspiring others with what you have achieved and demonstrating that you haven't lost the motivation to continue learning and improving too.

> The more powerful you are, the more your actions will have an impact on people, the more responsible you are to act humbly.

POPE FRANCIS
b. 1936

SOURCE: TED talk
DATE: April 2017
FIELD: Religion

Pope Francis was the first Latin American pope and the first from the southern hemisphere when elected to the position in March 2013. The former Archbishop of Buenos Aires, Argentinian cardinal Jorge Mario Bergoglio took the name Francis in honor of the Italian monk St. Francis of Assisi (ca. 1182–1226), whom he called "the man who gives us this spirit of peace, the poor man." As pope, he is known for his simple lifestyle, approachability, humility, and commitment to social justice. The quote opposite comes from an 18-minute talk he filmed in the Vatican and broadcast to the TED 2017 conference in Vancouver.

With power comes responsibility—the responsibility, Francis says, to act humbly. This insight echoes other quotes in the book about the need to put aside your ego as a leader and avoid the temptation to be proud of your achievements in an egoistical way. Pride is not bad in itself but it should be pride in the organization, in the excellence of your group's performance—the kind of pride that drives achievement, rather than the kind that encourages people to rest on their laurels and look down on others. Acting humbly means working alongside others, "getting your hands dirty," ensuring you understand your colleagues' needs and their position. Francis says, if you fail to be humble as leader you ruin not only "the other" but also yourself. It should be part of your commitment to excellence as a leader to be humble.

INDEX

absence 179
accountability 199
action 13, 45, 139, 165
Alexander the Great 21
anger 11, 33, 125
Aristotle 19
Arouet, François-Marie
  see Voltaire
authenticity 195
authority 31, 33, 79, 137, 183

Bacon, Sir Francis 41
Barenboim, Daniel 175
Blair, Tony 23, 145
Bowie, David 159
Bradman, Sir Don 107
Branson, Richard 153
Brown, Binta Niambi 197
Bryant, Kobe 199
Buchan, John 89
Buffett, Warren 173

Carnegie, Andrew 81
Carter, Rosalynn 135
challenges 27, 93, 113, 133
Charles the Great 35
Clinton, Bill 187
Comaneci, Nadia 133
commitment 75, 77, 121
communication 15, 141, 177
compassion 111
Confucius 13
connecting 77, 119

consensus 125, 135
control 61, 125, 163
counsellors 23
courage 67, 111, 113, 115
cowardice 169
creativity 131, 171, 175

Daodejing 9, 89
De Gaulle, Charles 117
delegation 71, 81, 99, 179
determination 95, 97, 105, 133
development 83, 113, 185, 193
Diogenes of Sinope 23
doubt 43, 67, 165
dynamism 115

education 13, 35, 181
Einstein, Albert 109
Elizabeth I 39
empathy 47, 63
empowerment 9, 71, 89, 143, 147
enriching the world 77

fairness 21, 33, 37, 39
fanaticism 105
Ferguson, Alex 183
Ford, Henry 87
Forster, E. M. 73
Francis, Pope 205
Frederick the Great 51

Gandhi, Indira 129
Gandhi, Mohandas 101, 103, 125

Garza, Alicia 201
Gates, Bill 143
Genghis Khan 37
goals 13, 159
Goethe, Johann Wolfgang von
  55
good practice 65, 103, 123
Gregory the Great 33
Guevara, Ernesto "Che" 119

Hemingway, Ernest 91
Herbert, George 45
Homer 7
hope 59, 121, 165
Huffington, Arianna 191
humanity 119
humbleness 205

improvement 177, 193
inclusivity 187
individuality 79, 127, 203
innovation 171, 175
intervention 57, 117
intuition 175, 189
Jobs, Steve 171
Jordan, Michael 161
judgment 25, 49

Keller, Helen 93
Kennedy, John F. 115
Kesey, Ken 123
King, Martin Luther, Jr. 125,
  135

King, Stephen 169
Kissinger, Henry 131
knowledge 41

Laozi 9
leading by example 7, 17, 101, 123
learning 183
Lee, Robert E. 61
legacies 151
Lincoln, Abraham 63
listening skills 91
living the message 155
Lloyd George, David 85
Lombardi, Vince 121

MacArthur, Douglas 111
Mandela, Nelson 89, 147
Maxwell, John C. 203
McGraw, John 79
militancy 75
modeling behavior 75, 123, 131, 133

Napoleon Bonaparte 51, 59
Nehru, Jawaharlal 103, 129
Nelson, Lord Horatio 57
"no," ability to say 145
Nooyi, Indra 177

Obama, Barack 59, 163, 165, 167, 197
obedience 19
opportunities 109, 115, 161, 195
originality 171, 175
Ovid 31

Pankhurst, Emmeline 75
Parks, Rosa 157
Parton, Dolly 151

passion 73, 83, 105, 197
Patton, General George 99
Pericles 15
Perón, Eva 105
Peter the Great 47
Phillips, Donald T. 185
Polybius 25
Powell, Colin 149
practice 133
praise 9, 29, 31
presenteeism 191
problem-solving 149
Publilius Syrus 27
Pythagoras 11

questions 49, 53, 159

Reagan, Ronald 141
reputation 37, 39, 173
resistance 101, 103, 125
responsibility 97, 169, 203
Ringelmann, Danae 195
risk-taking 51, 107, 131, 153
Roddick, Anita 155, 197
Roosevelt, Eleanor 113
Roosevelt, Theodore 71
Ruskin, John 65
Ruth, George Herman "Babe" 95

Sandberg, Sheryl 179
Schwarzkopf, Norman 163
second-guessing 159
self-belief 29, 69, 131, 137
self-control 61, 125
self-discipline 19, 29, 163, 183
self-doubt 43, 67, 165
self-improvement 177
self-questioning 159

selflessness 81, 107
setbacks 53, 87, 93
Shakespeare, William 43, 165
simplicity 109
sincerity 85, 195
Sklar, Rachel 193
Socrates 17
solutions 87, 89
Stevenson, Robert Louis 67
stillness 129
success 167
supportive behavior 31, 107

Tagore, Rabindranath 83, 183
teams, understanding 37, 47, 49, 79
Temujin see Genghis Khan
Teresa, Mother 135, 139
Thatcher, Margaret 137, 203
trust 55, 71, 99
truth 101, 103

upward mobility 201

Victoria, Queen 69
Virgil 29
vision 135, 141
Voltaire 49

Walker, Alice 167
Ward, William Arthur 127
Washington, George 53
Wilson, Woodrow 77
Winfrey, Oprah 189
work-life balance 177, 191
workplace cultures 65, 131, 191
worthiness 161, 163

Yousafzai, Malala 181

CREDITS

SHUTTERSTOCK
6 © EyeSeeMicrostock 12 © Morphart Creation 14 © Kamira 18 © MidoSemsem 20 © Netfalls Remy Musser 22 © Murat Tegmen 28 © Mark Fearon 30 © Santi S 32 © Jorisvo 36 © Vkilikov 46 © Dani Vincek 48 © Georgios Kollidas 50 © Morphart Creation 52 © Stocksnapper 56 © Morphart Creation 62 © Hein Nouwens 66 © Channarong Pherngjanda 70 © Optimarc 76 © Morphart Creation 80 © Everett Historical 90 © Morphart Creation 104 © David Carillet 140 © Mark Reinstein 146 © Mark Reinstein 154 © Denis Nata 156 © Gino Santa Maria 170 © Can Yesil 174 © Fosin 178 © Aleksandr Kurganov 180 © Alena Brozova 182 © Melis 184 © Studiovin 186 © Anthony Correia 190 © Stokkete 196 © Africa Studio 198 © Picsfive 202 © Praszkiewicz

ALAMY
8 © Lou-Foto / Alamy Stock Photo 38 © Alamy Stock Photo 64 © GL Archive / Alamy Stock Photo 86 © Ewing Galloway / Alamy Stock Photo 94 © Glasshouse Images / Alamy Stock Photo 100 © GL Archive / Alamy Stock Photo 110 © Alamy Stock Photo 120 © Grainger Historical Picture Archive / Alamy Stock Photo 128 © Pictorial Press Ltd / Alamy Stock Photo 162 © Alamy Stock Photo

THINKSTOCK
188 © Thinkstock

Unless listed here, all images are in the public domain.